Managing Commodity Price Risk

Managing Commodity Price Risk

A *Supply Chain Perspective*

Second Edition

George A. Zsidisin, Janet L. Hartley,
Barbara Gaudenzi, and Lutz Kaufmann

BEP BUSINESS EXPERT PRESS

Managing Commodity Price Risk: A Supply Chain Perspective, Second Edition

Copyright © Business Expert Press, LLC, 2017.

First published in 2012 by
Business Expert Press, LLC
222 East 46th Street, New York, NY 10017
www.businessexpertpress.com

ISBN-13: 978-1-63157-063-6 (paperback)
ISBN-13: 978-1-63157-064-3 (e-book)

Business Expert Press Supply and Operations Management Collection

Collection ISSN: 2156-8189 (print)
Collection ISSN: 2156-8200 (electronic)

Cover and interior design by Exeter Premedia Services Private Ltd., Chennai, India

Second edition: 2017

10 9 8 7 6 5 4 3 2 1

Printed in the United States of America.

To Nick, Lucas, and Blaise, for showing me the joys of fatherhood every day,
and Donna, for your love and patience with my humor.

To Glenn, thanks for our many fun-filled years together and
to Caleb—I am so proud of you!

To my beautiful daughters, Emma and Vittoria, with love.

To Anja, thanks for your love and support.

Abstract

Almost every organization is exposed to financial risk stemming from commodity price volatility. Risk exposure may be direct, from the prices paid for raw materials transformed into products sold to customers, or indirect, from higher energy and transportation costs. The purpose of this book is to provide a range of approaches that organizations can implement and adapt for managing commodity price volatility and reducing their exposure to the financial risks associated with purchased goods and services. This topic is important for supply chain and finance professionals owing to the significant direct financial effects price volatility has on profitability, organizational cash flow, the ability to competitively price products, new product design, buyer–supplier relationships, and the negotiation process.

Flexibility, a key competitive capability for managing supply chains, is likewise essential for managing commodity price risk. This book, which contains new content and updated examples relative to our first edition, provides supply chain managers a way to assess their organization's exposure to price risk. Based on the extent of risk and their organizations' risk appetites, supply chain and finance managers can choose from a range of options for effectively managing commodity price risk from direct commodity purchases, as well as exposure to risk from value chain purchases. The book will help supply chain and finance managers to develop and implement effective short- and long-term forecasts and to select the most appropriate risk management strategies for their organizations. Further, the decisions, actions, and policies taken today can significantly affect the options available for managing commodity price risk in the future. The viability and effectiveness of the overall risk management process and respective techniques are discussed, predominately from the buying-firm's perspective.

Keywords

commodity analysis, forecasting, hedging, market analysis, price volatility, risk management

Contents

Preface

Commodity price volatility and its inherent risk to profitability, costs, and availability is a supply chain challenge—and opportunity. Almost all businesses are exposed at some level to the financial risk stemming from commodity price volatility. Risk exposure may come from changes in direct materials prices, for example, wheat for a flour producer, aluminum for an automotive parts supplier, or plastic for a packaging producer. Indirect purchases such as utilities and transportation create price risk for many types of organizations including services. The greatest risk may be from purchases made by companies several tiers upstream in a supply chain, increasing the risk management challenge.

The commodity price risk management challenge transcends businesses and business functions and thus requires cross-functional and interorganizational perspectives. Commodity price volatility affects a number of strategic decisions including product design and development, product pricing, inventory management, negotiations, contracting, and managing supplier relationships. Supply chain management, which serves the critical role of managing product flows, finances, and information within and among firms, is in a prime position to provide a leadership role in managing the risk from commodity price volatility.

Objectives

The objective of this book is to provide supply chain and finance professionals an understanding of their organizations' exposure to commodity price risk, tools to forecast commodity prices in the short- and long-term, and approaches for managing risk exposure by the firm and within the supply chain. These approaches can be combined creating a flexible approach for managing commodity price risk. Several specific objectives of this second edition are for you to begin attaining the supply chain skill sets for the following:

- Understanding the importance of commodity price risk.
- Assessing organizational exposure to commodity price volatility.
- Forecasting short- and long-term commodity prices using technical and fundamental analysis.
- Incorporating enablers and inhibitors in the commodity price risk management decision process.
- Selecting the appropriate or set of appropriate commodity price risk management approaches for managing direct commodity purchases and value chain purchases.
- Gleaning insight to emerging issues of political risk, with the example of heavy rare earth metals, and business loans in China using commodities as collateral.
- Obtaining a greater appreciation for financial hedging instruments.

Structure

The book is organized into four sections: (1) background, (2) forecasting commodity prices, (3) managing commodity price risk, and (4) additional observations and cases.

Background

The Background section begins with Chapter 1—Introduction to Commodity Price Risk Management, which sets the stage for understanding the history and organizational challenges with and effects of commodity price volatility. Building from the first chapter, Chapter 2—Assessing Price Risk Exposure and Risk Tolerance, explains how to examine the extent of exposure, uncertainty, and an organization's risk tolerance when deciding whether or not it makes economic and strategic sense to actively manage risk. If you determine that price volatility should be managed, the next step is to develop short- and long-term price forecasts.

Forecasting Commodity Prices

Many of the approaches for managing commodity price volatility discussed in this book take time to create or implement, and are done in response to price forecasts. Chapter 3—Short-Term Forecasting, provides a series of tools and examples for developing short-term forecasts, usually from one week to several quarters in the future, using an approach called Technical Analysis. Chapter 4—Long-Term Forecasting, on the other hand, examines how to forecast for 1 year or more in the future by understanding the dynamics and effects of the supply–demand balance using Fundamental Analysis. Both these approaches are necessary for understanding how to manage commodity price volatility for both the short- and long-term.

Managing Commodity Price Risk

Chapter 5—Direct Purchases, provides an array of approaches, listed in order of complexity and resources to implement, to manage commodity price volatility when acquiring commodities in their "raw form." Organizational exposure to commodity price volatility, however, is not constrained only to direct purchases. As firms have become more specialized focusing on their core competencies, there is greater reliance on component and subassembly suppliers, many of which are exposed to commodity price volatility from their own raw material purchases. Chapter 6—Value Chain Purchases, explores approaches for managing commodity price volatility from suppliers. The insights from these two chapters are extended in the subsequent section on additional observations and cases.

Additional Observations and Cases

There are numerous examples of forecasting and management commodity price volatility throughout the book. This final section extends those examples by providing emerging supply chain challenges associated with commodity price volatility, and further insight to one of the management approaches discussed in the book. Chapter 7—Political Risk: The Case of

Heavy Rare Earth Metals, provides additional insights to political issues within global supply chains and how complex supply chains are managed. Increasing demand for electronic devices and newer technologies has increased demand for heavy rare earth metals, and China policies influence sourcing strategies. The following Chapter 8—Using Commodities as Collateral: The Case of China, examines how commodity price volatility influences an alternative form of financing—collateral loans using commodities. The concluding Chapter 9—Further Insights on Financial Hedging Instruments, goes into much further depth in the use of financial hedging instruments, as introduced in both Chapters 4 and 5.

Updates from the First Edition

The second edition of this book provides a significant change and, what we believe, is an improvement from the first edition. Prior to the first edition, we were not familiar with any work focusing on commodity price volatility from a supply chain perspective. With our emerging work in this field, in conjunction with content we provide to our students and managers about commodity price volatility, as a subset of cost analysis, we saw an opportunity to write our first book on the subject. Business Expert Press, and their mission to provide "deep dives" into specific business topics oriented to executive students, was perfectly aligned with our target audience. We appreciated the opportunity for publishing the first edition. However, in the four short years since the publication of the first book, much has changed; thus, it was important to significantly update and add content to the second edition.

Several of the specific updates include the changing structure of the book, providing new approaches and perspectives for managing commodity price risk, and incorporating a more global perspective of commodity price volatility.

Changing Structure

Now with nine chapters, the order of the chapters was changed to provide a more logical flow and greater clarity for understanding and managing commodity price risk. Further, within these changes, we have updated the data and examples in the short- and long-term forecasting chapters, as well as sources of information.

The chapter on currency exchange rate volatility in the first edition was not included in the second edition. While the topic of currency risk is important, we believe much more depth would be needed to effectively cover this topic, detracting from our primary focus on commodities. However, we would like to encourage other scholars and practitioners to examine currency exchange rate risk in greater depth and publish those insights.

In lieu of currency exchange rate risk, we elaborate more on specific issues and topics related to commodities. Hence our concluding section provides additional observations and cases focused on elements of commodity price volatility. This includes a discussion of political risk with the example of heavy rare earth metals in Chapter 7, and an interesting by-product effect on commodity price risk by its effect on using commodities as collateral for business loans in China in Chapter 8, contributed by Mr. Antonio Cesarano. In addition to these two chapters, we also included an invited contribution by Mr. Ugo Montagnini providing additional insights on financial hedging instruments in Chapter 9.

Providing New Approaches for Managing Commodity Price Risk

Another significant update to this edition is we have expanded the number of management approaches described. Since the publication of the first edition, we were honored to receive a CAPS Research Grant titled "Managing Commodity Price Volatility and Risk."[1] The CAPS Research study consisted of 12 in-depth case studies of firms based in the United States, Germany, and Italy, studying how they assess and manage commodity price risk exposure with their purchases and key supplier purchases. This edition captures several additional approaches discovered from the CAPS Research study, and we wish to thank Professor Phil Carter, CAPS Research, and the Institute for Supply Management for their support. Therefore, this edition provides additional approaches for managing commodity price risk, including building in financial slack, staggering contracts, and switching suppliers for direct commodity purchases, and creating firm fixed-price contracts, piggyback contracting, and vertically integrating for value chain purchases.

We realized in the prior edition we did not clearly differentiate commodity price risk management approaches by their source. Specifically, we did not provide clear guidance on which approaches to use if the price risk comes from commodities directly purchased or from the risk associated with component and assembly suppliers. Therefore, we split the prior "Creating a Commodity Price Risk Management Strategy" into two chapters, the current Chapter 5, "Managing Commodity Price Risk—Direct Purchases," and Chapter 6, "Managing Commodity Price Risk—Value Chain Purchases." We believe this change provides greater clarity with regard to selecting commodity price risk management approaches, especially with regard to the level of complexity and investments required for adopting such approaches.

Incorporating a Global Perspective

The four authors of this second edition have had the pleasure to work closely with each other studying commodity price volatility assessment and management during the past 5 years. Prior projects have included working in partnership on translating and updating material from the first edition in German[2] and Italian.[3] In addition, as previously described, we worked on a large-scale international study investigating commodity price risk assessment and management.[4] Throughout our work together we have had strong mutual desires for understanding this research phenomenon and managerial challenges from a global perspective. We believe the natural inclusion of Professors Gaudenzi and Kaufmann in this second edition adds significant value and a global perspective. This is further exemplified by including cases and perspectives from Italian practitioners managing commodity price volatility, as described in Chapters 8 and 9. Even throughout the manuscript we have provided more examples of assessment and management approaches from firms outside North America, as compared with the first edition. Commodity price risk and its management is truly global in scope, and this second edition incorporates a much-improved global perspective.

Acknowledgments

We would like to express our appreciation to all the people who have provided assistance and guidance to the development of this book. We want to thank Scott Isenberg and Charlene Kronstedt from Business Expert Press who made this revision possible. We would like to thank the companies that have contributed to our research and students in our programs for sharing their knowledge and experiences with us. Specifically, we would like to thank Dr. Phil Carter, CAPS Research, and the Institute for Supply Management, for their generous support of a grant to further support our study of commodity price volatility. We especially would like to thank Melanie Kulesz and Donna Greif for all their assistance in the formatting and organizing of this book.

SECTION I
Background

CHAPTER 1

Introduction to Commodity Price Risk Management

Why Is Commodity Price Risk Management Important?

Almost every organization is exposed to financial risk stemming from commodity price volatility. Risk exposure may be direct, from the prices paid for raw materials transformed into products sold to customers, or it may be indirect, from higher energy and transportation costs. The purpose of this book is to describe several approaches organizations can implement and adapt for managing commodity price volatility and reducing exposure to the financial risk associated with purchased goods and services. This topic is important for supply chain and finance professionals due to the significant direct financial effects price volatility has on profitability and organizational cash flow. The management of commodity price risk is also related to strategic decisions regarding—for example—product price positioning, new product design, buyer–supplier relationships, and negotiations.

Many commodities are subject to price volatility. The International Institute for Sustainable Development observed commodity prices are highly volatile in the short term, sometimes varying by as much as 50 percent in a single year.[1] One of its examples reported from 1983 to 1997 is the world-market prices for Robusta coffee beans moving between 40 and 195 percent from the average price. Despite continuous price fluctuations, Robusta coffee then faced a relatively stable price increase between 2004 and 2008, moving from a monthly price of 36.71 to 122.44 U.S. cents per pound. Since that period, the price has not been below 80 U.S. cents per pound,[2] with its price fluctuations strongly influenced by Brazilian economic performance and currency exchange rates.

From August 2003 to March 2004, world soybean prices rose from $237 to $413 per metric ton, an increase of 74 percent, and then fell back down to $256 per metric ton over the next 24 months. From June 2007 to June 2008 soybeans monthly prices had an almost continuous growth from $309.01 to $554.15 per metric ton, stimulated by the demand primarily from China. A similar increase occurred between December 2011 and August 2012, moving from $420.05 to $622.91 per metric ton. Prices then started decreasing, due to different factors such as Chinese market dynamics, new emerging competitors, and natural disasters affecting the quality of harvests. The U.S. Department of Agriculture (USDA) recently highlighted world soybean production in 2013 to 2015 was 318.95 million metric tons, with 319.61 million metric tons projected for 2015 to 2016.[3] In summary, many agricultural commodities are characterized by great volatility, with various fluctuations.

Looking at precious metals, the price of silver was traded at around $18 per ounce in April and May 2010, and less than a year later, it almost tripled in value to $49 per ounce during the final week of April 2011.[4] The year 2012 was highly volatile for most precious metals, with silver reaching an average price of $31.15 per ounce, the second highest price level on record, behind the average reached in 2011. Due to global silver investment strategies, demand for silver doubled in 2013, with an average price of $23.79 per ounce. The year 2014 remained very volatile, and 2015 was an extremely challenging year for all the commodities. In 2015, silver prices averaged $15.68 per ounce influenced by the continuing slowdown in the Chinese market and the stronger U.S. dollar.[5]

Commodity price movements affect almost every business organization not only in the form of raw material purchases and in components and subassemblies containing these commodities, but also in all the support activities necessary for firms to operate. Depending on the industry and form of products or services provided, many organizations are subject to the threats of commodity price volatility in the purchased products they acquire. Examples of these consist of the raw materials organizations transform into products, such as corn, wheat, and soy that are processed into the cereals consumers buy from retail stores; various metals such as copper, which is processed to make wiring; and petroleum by-products that are the key feedstocks in the plastics used in many products, equipment, and packaging materials. For example, a food products company such as Mondelez International is exposed to price risk from wheat, sugar, and cocoa used in its products; from paper and plastics used in its packaging materials; from natural gas used as energy in manufacturing; and from diesel fuel for transportation in its distribution network.[6]

Price volatility can also positively or negatively affect the product cost structures of an organization's suppliers. This subsequently influences the prices paid for the multitude of products, subassemblies, components, packaging, equipment, and services sourced by firms. The ability of suppliers to manage price volatility can further influence their ability to meet customers' requirements. If these price fluctuations are not well managed, issues such as requests for price increases, delays, and even supply disruptions can result, detrimentally affecting the overall cost structures and sourcing options of purchasing firms.

Although most firms are directly exposed to commodity price volatility in their purchases from suppliers, just about every organization encounters this price risk indirectly. For example, the transportation costs of shipping products are partly dependent on the diesel and jet fuel prices. Natural gas and electricity are often consumed and applied as overhead costs for producing products and services, and in the utilities consumed for office operations. Thus, most organizations—whether they are manufacturing-based, service-oriented, for- or not-for-profit, or governmental agencies—are exposed to commodity price volatility and risk. The following two brief examples provide some initial insights as to the effects of commodity price volatility.

Downside of Price Volatility

Commodity price volatility impacts profitability in many different industries. One interesting example of commodity price volatility concerns the McDonald's Corporation and the costs associated with acquiring food. In January 2011, McDonald's had predicted 2 to 3 percent inflation in food prices.[7] A large percentage of the McDonald's Corporation's operating profits come from its franchises and royalties, protecting it somewhat from the price volatility in commodities such as beef and wheat used in its products and paper used in packaging. Individual McDonald's franchises directly purchasing food might have a more difficult time dealing with rising commodity prices. As fast-food customers are conscious consumers, they may balk at product-price increases. Thus rising commodity prices could eventually hurt profits of the overall corporation if prices rise to levels making it difficult for franchises to expand.

Another more dramatic example of the potential effects of commodity price volatility concerns Skybus Airlines, a low-cost airline based out of Columbus, Ohio.[8] Skybus Airlines was forced to file for bankruptcy in 2008 because it was unable to keep up with rising fuel costs, a situation exacerbated by the slowing economy. Fuel costs can account for 30 to 40 percent of an airline's overall costs.[9] For start-up firms with limited capital, missing budget projections because of commodity price increases can be devastating.

These are two of many examples of organizations having to cope with commodity price volatility. In the first example, we see volatile food prices can affect McDonald's franchises' profitability and growth potential. However, the financial losses anticipated at McDonald's pales in comparison to the example of Skybus Airlines, where commodity price volatility became a significant contributor to the financial disaster and dissolution of the firm.

Commodity price fluctuations are usually outside of the control of any one firm because the forces of market demand and supply often transcend industries, technologies, and countries. However, organizations can still plan for and mitigate the effects of these price movements in order to improve overall business performance. Thus, supply chain managers must develop and implement strategies to reduce the negative impact of price volatility on their organization's performance. However, commodity price volatility also provides opportunities for success. Organizations that effectively manage the risk from commodity price volatility can improve performance by enriching the financial bottom line, leveling cash flow in budgeting, enhancing value in product and process design, and better preparing for negotiations.

Creating Value from Price Volatility

Organizations can attain a competitive advantage by understanding and effectively managing price risk. Simply stated, a dollar saved in purchase prices is a dollar going directly to the bottom line. Further, savings in purchase prices result in lower inventory valuations due to a lower purchase price, so a company's assets are lower. Higher revenues and lower inventory valuations improve key corporate financial metrics such as return on assets (ROA), as described in the strategic profit model, also called the DuPont model.[10] This reason alone should provide strong incentives for firms to manage commodity price risk because it directly improves the overall profitability of their organizations by potentially reducing the overall prices paid for purchased goods and services, including those commodities subject to price volatility. For example, in the late 1990s and early 2000s, Southwest Airlines' ability to successfully manage fuel price risk helped it to be profitable while other airlines struggled.[11] In recent years, most airlines experienced—or are now experiencing—a strong correlation between jet fuel price dynamics and their performances and returns. A study published in 2015 highlighted how companies in the airline industry are increasingly investing in several risk mitigation strategies, particularly financial hedging.[12]

Understanding commodity price volatility is essential for effective budgeting. Organizations typically develop operating budgets a year or more into the future. When developing operating budgets, cross-functional teams use forecasts of customer demand and input costs to make pricing decisions and profitability projections. The ability to forecast short- and long-term commodity prices and to apply appropriate strategies can increase stability in firms' cost structures. Although some price movements may still occur, firms can make a more accurate assessment of future purchase costs. This can allow the marketing and sales function, for example, to more accurately estimate and negotiate prices with customers for longer-term commitments while ensuring profitability.

Commodity price volatility can spur creativity in the product and design processes. Companies may use value analysis or value engineering. Value analysis involves the systematic analysis of identifying and selecting the best value alternatives for designs, materials, processes, and systems. It proceeds by repeatedly asking, "Can the cost of this item or step be reduced or eliminated without diminishing effectiveness, required quality, or customer satisfaction?" While value analysis generally refers to this process after the product has been launched, value engineering occurs while the product is still being designed. Its objectives are to distinguish between the incurred costs (actual use of resources) and the inherent costs (locked in) in a particular design, as well as to minimize the locked-in costs.

The analysis and management of price risk can have a direct effect on providing value to customers and should be taken into consideration in value analysis/engineering activities. For example, between 2004 and 2006 the European Commission supported the Polycoat project to develop innovative cost-effective and eco-friendly steel packaging cans and to research alternative raw materials to reduce costs and price volatility exposure.[13] In another example, the instability of petroleum prices created momentum for firms to consider developing alternatives to the traditional plastic "clamshell packaging." As a result, MeadWestvaco (now WestRock) developed a packaging product called "Natralock," which consists of a tamper-evident cardboard sheet originally supplied for pharmaceutical trials.[14] The package reduces plastic by 60 percent, on average, versus the clamshell version for a given product, reducing materials' costs. It also is lighter by 30 percent, which cuts down on transportation costs and fuel use. Therefore, significant commodity price movements can potentially serve as a catalyst for designing new products, features, or production processes in order to be more cost-effective and still meet customer requirements.

Firms preparing for negotiations with suppliers or customers can benefit from thoroughly assessing and providing strong supporting evidence for managing commodity price risk. Several purposes for conducting a thorough commodity price analysis in preparation for negotiations include:

- Estimating the overall potential risk suppliers and customers encounter from commodity price movements and to explore how risk can be best managed.
- Providing commodity price information used in deriving overall cost estimates and ranges in negotiating prices with suppliers and customers.
- Creating clear expectations of how commodity price volatility risk can affect the overall ability of the supplier to successfully

fulfill an organization's purchase requirements, which should be a major factor in the overall supplier selection decision.

Commodity price analysis is an important tool for better estimating cost structures and conducting what-if analyses in preparing for negotiations with suppliers and customers. The analyses can be applied in understanding the cost drivers of supplier products, as well as in deriving cost estimates and ranges in supporting and negotiating proposed prices to customers. There are numerous factors to consider when negotiating with suppliers or customers regarding commodity price volatility. One factor to consider during negotiations is what actions and capabilities, if any, the other party is taking to manage price risk. There may be circumstances where a supplier is planning to use financial hedging to offset its raw material purchase-price fluctuations. As a result, a customer of this supplier may have little need to develop specific strategies for managing price risk, as long as the financial risk exposure of the commodity is appropriately hedged throughout the life of the contract. These issues can be explored during the preparation and initial information exchange phases of the negotiation, which can include estimating materials usage, analyzing price movements, and determining effective strategies for managing commodity price risk.

Alternatively, many suppliers may not have the resources necessary to mitigate their exposure to commodity price fluctuations due to a variety of reasons such as firm size, purchase size, expertise in supply management, or influence with their suppliers. As a result, if the supplier excels in other characteristics, such as engineering expertise or quality, it makes sense to explore other means to offset the risk of price movements, such as piggybacking off of the company's contracts in the purchase of the commodity or inserting escalator clauses in the contracts to share risk with the supplier. Negotiations with suppliers or customers over how the price risk associated with commodities is managed may depend on the buying strength of the firms; the influence the firms have on the other party; the purchaser of the commodity; the length of the contract; the quantity and overall value of the commodity as a percentage of spend or product price; and the ability to change specifications.

Supply chain managers in every organization need to understand how to effectively assess and manage price risk. By effectively managing price risk, they can reduce negative consequences and take advantage of opportunities to improve performance.

Overview of the Book

The purpose of this book is to provide a flexible process you can use for managing commodity price risk for your organization. Chapters 1 and 2 provide background to the supply chain challenge of commodity price volatility. All supply chain and finance managers need to assess their organization's level of exposure to price risk to determine if it is worthwhile to invest resources to manage risk. Chapter 2 explains how to assess your organization's risk exposure and the effect an organization's risk tolerance can have on managing commodity price volatility. The second section of the book provides an overview of processes and tools supply chain and finance professionals can employ to forecast commodity prices. If your firm is vulnerable to commodity price volatility, forecasting short- and long-term commodity prices are necessary for determining if proactive management of that risk is necessary, as well as the most appropriate approaches to pursue. Chapter 3, in particular, describes how to use technical analysis based on historical price patterns to develop a short-term price forecast. Long-term forecasts are developed by thoroughly understanding the relationship between the commodity's supply and its demand, as described in Chapter 4.

The third section of the book delves into approaches firms can implement and tailor for best managing commodity price risk exposure. From the information attained in assessing risk exposure and forecasting commodity prices, Chapter 5 provides guidelines and approaches, listed in order of complexity, for managing commodity price risk associated with direct purchases. Chapter 6 likewise provides managerial guidance for approaches to manage commodity price risk, but instead its focus is toward the risk associated with supplier purchases, which we label as value chain purchases.

The final section of the book provides several cases, additional examples, and other insights of commodity price volatility and how firms assess and manage this form of supply risk. Chapter 7 examines political risk and its influence on commodity price volatility with the examples of heavy rare earth metals and conflict metals. We are grateful for the contributions from those in supply chain practice who have shared their experiences and approaches with us. In Chapter 8, Mr. Antonio Cesarano of MPS Capital Services provides insight to the interesting case of using commodities as collateral in China, and the respective challenges associated with this practice. Chapter 9, written by Mr. Ugo Montagnini of MPS Capital Services, extends the initial insights of hedging with financial instruments, as initially introduced in Chapter 5.

CHAPTER 2

Assessing Price Risk Exposure and Risk Tolerance

As described in Chapter 1, commodity price volatility affects almost all organizations, either directly through their own purchases, or indirectly through their supply chains. Since commodity prices are usually outside the control of any one organization, supply chain professionals are rarely able to directly influence commodity prices. Instead, supply chain managers must understand their organizations' exposure to price risk and decide if, and how, their organization should manage commodity price risk. Chapters 3 and 4 will explain how to analyze price movements and develop forecasts if the risk exposure warrants direct attention. Chapters 5 and 6 describe a variety of approaches for managing price risk for direct commodity purchases and value chain purchases, respectively, and when they are likely to be most effective. It is tempting to "jump right in" and begin using these approaches immediately. However, the successful implementation of many of these approaches takes time and can require a significant amount of organizational resources. For example, research is necessary for developing a deep understanding of a commodity to forecast its price movements in the short- and long-term, as explained in Chapters 3 and 4. Further, many of the risk management approaches require close cooperation and collaboration among departments within an organization and with other supply chain members. Thus, it is important to first assess your organization's degree of exposure to commodity price risk and the risk tolerance of your management team before implementing risk management approaches.

In this chapter, we describe how to assess an organization's exposure to price risk, its risk tolerance, and an approach for setting risk management objectives. The first step consists of estimating the firm's overall exposure to commodity price volatility. This is determined by understanding the overall dependence of the firm on the commodity and the extent of volatility commodity prices exhibit. The importance of understanding corporate and business unit risk tolerance is examined. We explain how to set risk objectives providing direction as to which price risk management approaches may be congruent with the firm's overall strategy, philosophical orientation, and capabilities.

Estimate Overall Risk Exposure

Almost all organizations are exposed to commodity price risk, typically from a number of different types of commodities. Supply chain managers need to assess the commodities their organization purchases, the degree of price risk exposure from each, and determine how to deploy their organization's resources to attain the greatest financial benefit. Two key factors determine an organization's exposure to commodity price risk: (a) the organization's level of dependence on the commodity and (b) the extent of volatility in the commodity's prices. As shown in Figure 2.1, if the level of dependence and price volatility are low, it is best to monitor the situation to stay current on potential new developments with the commodity's market and not actively manage price risk. This is because the cost of actively managing price risk will outweigh its financial benefits. As dependence and price volatility increase, active management of price risk can have a positive impact on financial performance. Thus firms should apply

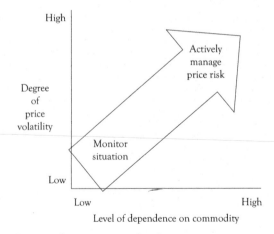

Figure 2.1 Price risk exposure and risk management

the risk management approaches most appropriate to their situation, as discussed in Chapters 5 and 6.

Assess Dependence

Assessing an organization's exposure to price risk requires determining how dependent an organization is on the commodity. Organizational dependence is determined by the amount of the commodity an organization purchases directly, the amount purchased by upstream suppliers, and the flexibility and ease of substituting one commodity for another.

The process begins by conducting an internal spend analysis. A spend analysis identifies how much an organization is spending on which commodities, by which organizational units, from which suppliers, and at what prices.[1] The spend analysis should include direct purchases in the bill of materials of the organization's products and indirect purchases such as energy and transportation. Some commodities may be both a direct and an indirect purchase. For example, natural gas influences the price of plastics used in many different products and packaging materials both directly and indirectly. Figure 2.2 shows how natural gas is used both as an energy source and an upstream raw material for producing high-density polyethylene (HDPE) plastics used to make a wide range

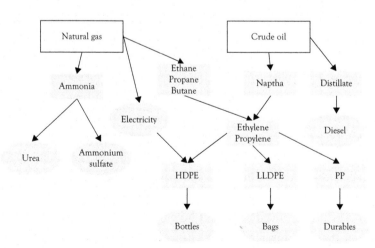

Figure 2.2 The influence of natural gas and crude oil price movements on plastics[2]

of products including bottles, pipes, and plastic sheets. Thus natural gas price increases can affect the price of HDPE in two ways.

For some organizations and commodities, doing a spend analysis may be a relatively easy task. For example, most trucking companies can easily measure how much they are spending on diesel fuel each year, and a cereal manufacturer should have a good understanding of how much corn they purchase each year. For other companies and commodities, doing the spend analysis can actually be quite a complex undertaking. Many firms have a multitude of products, production plants or service centers, and business units. It is possible that although each product only uses a small amount of a certain commodity, across the entire company the total commodity spend could be significant, exposing the company to price risk. The knowledge of how much is spent within each of the units may or may not be readily visible at the corporate level, especially in organizations with decentralized organizational structures. Corporate-wide enterprise resource planning (ERP) systems increase the availability of spend data and many e-procurement systems include modules for spend analysis. In addition, spend analysis can be done using spreadsheets or specialized software.

In addition to direct purchases, commodities are embedded in parts, components, products, and services an organization purchases from its suppliers. For example, an organization can both acquire copper as a raw material, as well as purchase parts made of copper from suppliers (i.e., wiring harnesses). What happens if copper prices increase? Some of copper's price risk may already be managed (in part) by having firm, fixed contract prices with suppliers for the wiring harnesses (one of the management approaches discussed in Chapter 6). Even if the firm is not immediately affected by the increase in price of copper from the wiring harness supplier, if the price of copper becomes too steep, and the supplier itself does not proactively manage its exposure to copper price increases, the supplier experiences financial difficulties and may request price increases. Even if some of the upstream commodity spend from suppliers is temporarily protected from price increases, it becomes imperative to know how and when those circumstances may change—and whether additional measures are needed to manage risk. Thus, firms need to understand which commodities are used to a large amount within your organization and in the supply chain. This requires working closely with first-tier suppliers to understand their exposure to commodity risk and how risk is being managed. In addition, visibility upstream into the supply chain is needed to identify sources of risk from suppliers beyond the first tier.

The results of the overall spend analysis helps to determine if it even makes sense to actively pursue the risk management approaches described in this book. For example, if a firm has revenues of $2 billion with a cost of goods sold of $1 billion, but only has an overall average annual spend of $10,000 for a commodity, even a 100 percent price increase will most likely have minimal impact on profitability.

In addition to helping identify the degree of price risk exposure, understanding the overall commodity spend in the supply chain is necessary for implementing some of the risk management approaches. For example, developing favorable contractual clauses with suppliers or customers requires an understanding of overall anticipated spend and should be integrated with the overall sourcing strategy pursued by the organization.

To implement financial hedging using, for example, futures contracts requires estimating actual forecasted requirements in order to offset the appropriate amount of risk exposure of the commodity. Hedging involves the use of financial instruments such as futures contracts or options, such as those traded in the Chicago Mercantile Exchange (CME). Futures contracts are only sold in specified quantities for each contract, as discussed in Chapter 5. For example, contracts for Henry Hub natural gas futures are bought and sold in quantities of 10 million British thermal units (BTU).[3] If the spend exposure for the firm is less than what is required to obtain a futures contract, then this technique for managing commodity price volatility would not be viable for the firm. Pooling together commodity requirements among the various products produced, production facilities, and business units can allow organizations to leverage their overall commodity requirements and utilize a broader range of price risk management approaches, such as financial hedging.

An organization's dependence on a commodity is also affected by the organization's ability to quickly and easily substitute another commodity for the same purpose. Either aluminum or copper can be used in wiring; packaging materials can be plastic or paper; and building materials can be plastic or plywood. If production processes are flexible, and customers are either open to the change or the change is not visible to customers, an organization can switch between commodities depending on price. However, relevant investments in research and development and market research may be needed to determine if substitution is technically and commercially viable. The price risk management approach of substitution is discussed in greater detail in Chapter 5.

Determine Degree of Price Volatility

As shown in Figure 2.1, the second factor affecting an organization's risk exposure is the extent of commodity price volatility. If historically a commodity's prices have not varied much and no major changes are expected in the future, exposure to price risk is low. In this case the situation should be monitored, but proactive management of price risk is not needed. Therefore, it is important to know if the price movements of a commodity actually have an effect on the firm now or in the future. Unforeseen natural disasters or political events such as hurricanes, earthquakes, war, or political strategies can affect commodity prices. However, the probability of such an event occurring in any given time frame is very low.

There are several techniques you can use to assess the amount of variation in commodity prices. One is to simply calculate the standard deviation of published weekly or monthly commodity prices over a year or greater period. If the overall standard deviation is relatively low in comparison with the mean (average) prices, then price volatility may not be a significant issue. Should you use weekly or monthly prices for this assessment? The time interval of weekly or monthly prices should be consistent with the frequency of commodity purchases, particularly from the spot market. If your organization usually acquires the commodity in weekly or more frequent shipments, then analyzing weekly price movements is appropriate. If the purchase schedules occur less frequently, then monthly data may be more appropriate.

Note longer time intervals typically show lower levels of price volatility because of the effect of averaging. For example, compare weekly and monthly natural gas spot prices (US$/million BTU) for 2015 at the

Henry Hub delivery point. Analysis of data published by the U.S. Energy Information Administration[4] is shown in Table 2.1. The minimum price is lower, the maximum price is higher, and the standard deviation is higher when the analysis is done using weekly prices, as compared to monthly prices. However, whether weekly or monthly data are used, an analysis of the standard deviation alone does not provide a complete picture of risk exposure.

Another technique for estimating price risk is to take the range of monthly prices (highest minus lowest observed price) in a year divided by the mean price of the commodity. This provides information with regard to the percentage change in the price of the commodity in relation to its average annual price. Table 2.2 shows an analysis of average monthly prices for natural gas (US$/1,000 cubic ft.) at the wellhead for the years 2006 through 2015. Note wellhead prices are different than the spot prices quoted at the Henry Hub and are in different units. To do the analysis, the minimum and maximum monthly prices throughout each respective year were first determined. Then the range (highest minus lowest price) was calculated for each year and divided by the overall monthly average for each year. This number was then multiplied by 100 to convert the number to a percentage.

The information in Table 2.2 shows significant price fluctuations for natural gas. The average annual price movement is 30.5 percent from 2006 until 2015, with a high of over 52.9 percent in 2006 and a low of almost 20 percent in 2012. In this example we see, as long as spend levels warrant direct intervention, it would make sense to proactively manage the commodity price volatility of natural gas due to its significant price movements.

Table 2.1 Variation in weekly and monthly natural gas spot prices for 2015[5]

Time interval	Minimum price (US$/million BTU)	Maximum price (US$/million BTU)	Standard deviation (US$/million BTU)
Weekly prices	$1.68	$3.13	$0.35
Monthly prices	$1.93	$2.99	$0.33

Table 2.2 Estimating price risk: monthly wellhead prices (US$/1,000 cubic ft.)

Year	High	Low	Average	Percent from average (%)
2015	4.65	3.68	4.27	22.7
2014	6.57	4.91	5.70	29.1
2013	5.74	4.52	5.07	24.1
2012	5.13	4.19	4.71	20.0
2011	6.19	5.03	5.73	20.2
2010	6.84	5.48	6.07	22.4
2009	7.97	5.37	6.14	42.4
2008	12.48	7.80	9.59	48.8
2007	8.79	7.00	8.06	22.2
2006	10.80	6.42	8.28	52.9
			Overall	30.5

Source: U.S. Energy Information Administration.[6]

Understanding Risk Tolerance and Setting Risk Objectives

After understanding the level of price risk your organization is exposed to, the next step is to assess your organization's risk tolerance. Organizations have different levels of tolerance when it comes to the extent of risk they are willing to take in managing their supply chains and commodity spend. Risk tolerance depends on factors such as the firm's philosophy, history, industry, stage of products in the product life cycle, customer base, experiences, and corporate leadership, to name a few. An organization's risk tolerance can be generally viewed on a continuum from being risk averse, to risk neutral, to having a high-risk appetite, as shown in Figure 2.3.

Risk aversion refers to those firms preferring to engage in activities or decisions having a more certain outcome but lower returns, as compared with choices having less certain outcomes but higher expected value payouts. Likewise, organizations with a high-risk appetite are characterized by having a willingness to accept risk exposure and potentially adverse impacts from an event. As discussed by Cary[7] and provided in Table 2.3,

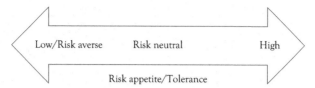

Figure 2.3 Commodity price-risk appetite and tolerance

Table 2.3 Questions for analyzing risk appetite

Where do we feel we should allocate our limited time and resources to minimize risk exposures? Why?
What level of risk exposure requires immediate action? Why?
What level of risk requires a formal response strategy to mitigate the potentially material impact? Why?
What events have occurred in the past, and at what level were they managed? Why?

there are several questions that can provide insight to an organization's risk tolerance and appetite.

The strategies you decide to pursue in addressing commodity price volatility need to be congruent with those of the business unit, the corporation, or both. For example, through market intelligence and forecasting, assume you estimate the spot price for a key commodity your organization purchases will increase by 10 percent in the next year. If your organization has a high-risk appetite, this potential price increase may not be considered significant enough to warrant actively managing price risk. However, if your organization is more risk averse you may be more inclined to manage price risk. Therefore, close coordination is necessary with a firm's leadership team in determining which risk management approaches are appropriate for the situation.

As shown in Table 2.4, organizations should consider several factors when setting risk objectives. As commodity prices fluctuate, there may be times when commodity market prices are favorable for an organization. It could be spot market prices are lower than the prices used in budgeting or contract prices with suppliers are below market prices. In these circumstances, the immediate risk exposure may be low and no additional actions, other than continuing to monitor the market, are necessary. As the old adage goes, "Do not fix it if it is not broken."

Table 2.4 Setting risk objectives

Do current commodity market prices represent a "value"?
What are the underlying commodity market fundamental trends?
Is there product price flexibility?
Can the business withstand potential margin erosion?
Is the changing price a blip or a long-term trend?

A second factor to take into consideration in setting risk objectives concerns understanding the market fundamentals of the commodity. As discussed in depth in Chapter 4, fundamental analysis consists of conducting a thorough analysis of what factors influence the overall supply and overall demand of a commodity—and whether or not those factors influence the price of the commodity. This requires gathering market intelligence from multiple sources, which involves taking a holistic snapshot of industry trends; understanding other industries having an influence on commodity demand, supply, and price; examining technological developments; and being aware of political and governmental interventions.

The price movement of silicon during 2006 is a classical case in this regard. For many years, semiconductor manufacturers enjoyed relatively low prices for polysilicon.[8] Then supply-market events, in conjunction with new customers from different industries who began using polysilicon, significantly changed the market's dynamics. First, the purchase of 51 percent of the ownership of Komatsu by Sumco[9] shifted the power base of the supply market, so two companies (Sumco and Shin-Etsu Chemical SHE) each had over 30 percent of the overall production capacity. Second, the solar energy industry started to emerge as a large consumer of polysilicon, partly instigated by government grants to develop solar technology as an alternate energy source. This new customer base for significant quantities of polysilicon affected the overall market by increasing demand for polysilicon. Further, from the semiconductor industry perspective, the solar industry has lower quality requirements, and due to the assistance of governmental grants, was not as price sensitive. The emergence of the solar industry helped spur the combined demand (solar and semiconductor) for polysilicon in 2006 to 40,564 metric tons, which exceeded the polysilicon manufacturing capability of 38,680 metric tons.[10] These industry and market effects increased polysilicon prices from $60 to $62 per kilogram, to $80 per kilogram for the semiconductor industry, and up to $200 to $250 per kilogram for solar energy applications. Therefore, understanding market fundamentals including the issues associated with consolidations, buy-outs, and the emergence of new customers in different industries can offer insight to potential price movements and provide key information for setting risk objectives.

In addition, we found, in several cases, organizations might differently interpret the abovementioned market trends, and might evaluate their risk exposure in different ways. For example, organizations in the bakery product industry have commonalities in terms of exposure to raw material price volatility. However, the different types of finished products they sell, the specific market positioning (in terms of final price and brand image), and their trade policies can lead to different perceptions of the risks. These aspects significantly influence the analysis of market fundamentals, the measure of risk exposure, and hence the adoption of mitigation approaches.

Setting risk objectives should not only be confined to the supply chain function, but should also encompass all key business functions and pertinent supply chain partners for developing an overall commodity price management strategy. Product price flexibility consists of the capacity and desire of the firm to change the prices of their products in relation to commodity price movements. If the price of the purchased raw materials increases for a commodity by $1.00, can the organization increase the product's sales price to customers to maintain its margins and offset the overall cost increase? This product price flexibility may not necessarily apply to all products sold or to all customers; and therefore, it is imperative to understand the overall exposure and vulnerability of the organization to determine how much flexibility it has to change prices. For example, your organization may already have a firm, fixed price contract with a customer; thus, it would be very difficult to pass price increases on to that respective customer. However, the higher commodity prices can be considered when negotiating contracts with new customers.

Several of the factors in Table 2.4 interact with each other when setting risk objectives. For example, the ability of a firm to withstand potential margin erosion can be significantly affected by whether the price change is a short-term blip or a long-term trend. If the price increase is a long-term trend, the duration of the increase is an important factor. The monthly prices of crude oil for 2006 until 2016 illustrate how commodity price movements can include both short-term blips and long-term trends. As shown in Figure 2.4, from 2007 to 2008 prices increased sharply, which has been attributed to market fundamentals of surging demand and falling supply.[11] Further, the 2008 price spike has been attributed to the role of speculation in the trading of crude oil futures contracts by several sources;[12] although counterarguments have been made, it may have been a congruence of events outside of speculation causing this price spike. The sharp price decline beginning in October 2008 was a result of the global recession, which was followed by price increases in 2009 with the gradual economic recovery. Prices were relatively stable in 2010 until March 2011 when protests and political upheaval in Libya and other areas in North Africa raised supply concerns.[13] Another price spike occurred in early 2012, attributed to potential supply disruptions in the Middle East.[14] The dramatic drop in oil prices beginning in 2014 is attributed to over supply from increased North American and Iraq production and other countries such as Saudi Arabia continuing their production, coupled with slowing demand in Europe and China.[15] Since June 2014, the oil market faced a strong downward price adjustment, which continued throughout 2015.

Short-term blips in price changes, such as those experienced with crude oil in 2008, are generally difficult to identify beforehand. Further, because they are generally short-term in duration, organizations are not

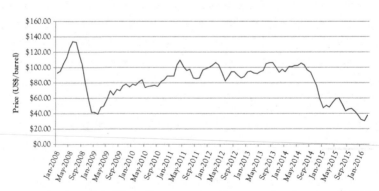

Figure 2.4 Monthly West Texas intermediate crude oil prices (US$/ barrel), 2002 to 2016

Source: U.S. Energy Information Administration.[16]

likely to have the flexibility to rapidly alter their strategies in managing these price spikes before and after they occur. However, if short-term changes in commodity valuations can be quickly identified, and there is some degree of flexibility, such as with product requirements and scheduling, inventory levels, and financial liquidity, there may be an opportunity to take temporary advantage of those price movements. For example, if there is reason to believe there is an imminent price spike, an organization, if it has the financial wherewithal and physical stock capability, can purchase the commodity in larger quantities (forward buy) in order to avoid paying the higher future price. If the commodity valuation is currently experiencing a price spike, and if the organization has sufficient levels of the commodity in inventory, it can attempt to "ride out" the abnormal price and wait until prices decrease to normal levels before repurchasing. However, this strategy is very difficult to execute from a logistics, financial, and organizational strategy perspective unless the flexibility mechanisms are in place and considered to be cost-effective, given the potential organizational savings.

Returning back to understanding whether commodity price movements are a short-term blip or a long-term trend, it is imperative for firms to identify through market intelligence those factors temporarily affecting short-term prices as well as long-term pattern shifts and trends. Taking advantage of short-term price movements is difficult and requires a significant degree of flexibility. On the other hand, flexible organizations will often have more options to implement strategies to better manage long-term commodity price movements.

Summary

In Chapter 2, we have explored the role of gathering intelligence, both internally with regard to understanding risk tolerance and assessing overall risk exposure, as well as externally, in terms of market dynamics and relationships in the supply chain. These issues help us identify whether or not you need to take proactive measures to manage commodity price volatility, as well as to provide guidance to the most appropriate approaches and techniques to implement when direct intervention is warranted. The results of the short- and long-term price forecasts discussed in forthcoming Chapters 3 and 4, in conjunction with the insights provided in Chapter 2, provide the impetus for proactively managing commodity price risk for direct commodity purchases, as out-lined in Chapter 5, and for value chain purchases (supplier commodity purchases) in Chapter 6.

SECTION II
Forecasting Commodity Prices

CHAPTER 3

Forecasting Short-Term Commodity Prices

Short- and long-term commodity price forecasts help you to make better risk management decisions. Long-term forecasts are looking out in the future, one year or more. Short-term forecasts look ahead to the next few weeks, months, or quarters.

In this chapter, we describe how to use technical analysis to develop short-term forecasts, and in Chapter 4, we discuss long-term forecasts. Technical analysis reviews historical price patterns, and forecasts are based on assumptions about future price patterns. The only data used in technical analysis are historical prices. The theory supporting technical analysis suggests all marketplace information about a commodity is incorporated into its price. As soon as new information is available about a commodity, the market adjusts to determine a new price. This underlying premise is attributed to Charles Dow,[1] who observed price patterns in the stock market. Dow suggested prices reflect factual information, as well as the expectations and beliefs of all market participants. Therefore, in a technical analysis there is no need for understanding the underlying factors affecting price dynamics; the analysis only uses the price's historical patterns.

Long-term forecasting uses an approach called fundamental analysis, which we discuss in Chapter 4. Fundamental analysis assumes the relationship between supply and demand drives commodity prices. Fundamental analysis involves examining the underlying forces affecting supply and demand, estimating how supply and demand will change, and then assessing what impact the change might have on price.

Managers use short-term forecasts to make tactical decisions to execute supply chain strategies. How are short-term price forecasts used in the company? For example, based on a price forecast, adjustments can be made on how much and when to buy a commodity. If a commodity's price is expected to increase, it can be acquired sooner than planned, and if prices are forecast to decrease, can be purchased at a later time. The time frame of these decisions determines the time period for short-term forecasts. Typically, monthly or weekly prices are used when forecasting near-term commodity prices. In our research, for example, we found in 85 percent of the companies, the forecasting frequency is monthly, and in only one case daily prices are used for the forecast. These choices are also influenced by the fact, for many commodities, it is easy to find monthly prices published by external sources. Quarterly or annual price forecasts are also available, but these are then typically used for long-term timeline forecasts.

With shorter time periods, say daily versus weekly prices, there can be a lot of variation in the forecast. Longer time periods, such as quarters, tend to smooth out price variations. If orders are placed infrequently, and the spend level and volatility are relatively low, quarterly or monthly forecasts may be more appropriate. In case of frequent purchases, high levels of spend, and highly volatile prices, developing weekly price forecasts may be a better choice.

The key steps in a technical analysis are described as follows:

1. Gathering historical commodity price data.
2. Identifying price patterns.
3. Selecting a forecasting model.
4. Developing forecasts for the appropriate price pattern (stable, trends, seasonality).
5. Developing forecasts for price patterns with trends.
6. Developing forecasts for seasonal price patterns.
7. Assessing forecast accuracy.
8. Improving the forecast.
9. Monitoring the forecast.

Gathering Historical Commodity Price Data

The first step in technical analysis is to gather historical commodity spot prices for the most recent two to three years. Spot prices are the actual prices paid in the marketplace during a given time period. Companies may have historical records on the actual prices paid for commodities. If price data are not readily available within the company, public sources or subscription services may be available. For example, gasoline, oil, natural gas, and coal prices are publicly available through the U.S. Energy Information Administration. The U.S. Department of Agriculture Economic Research Service provides price data for a number of agricultural commodities including corn, soybeans, and wheat; and the World Bank provides price data on a large number of commodities. Subscription services can be expensive but provide forecasts and market information as well, so they may be a valuable investment for your company. When using historical data from different sources, it is important to ensure they are consistent in terms of grade of the commodity, unit of measure, and time frame. For example, there are six different major classes of wheat, each with different producing regions, varying uses, and consuming countries.[2]

Identifying Price Patterns

The next step in a technical analysis is to plot the historical price data and identify patterns. This can be done using a spreadsheet plotting the price data for the most recent two to three years in a line graph in the order of occurrence. This is typically represented as a time-series price chart. The monthly wellhead natural gas prices for 2014 to 2016 from the U.S. Energy Information Administration shown in Table 3.1 are plotted in Figure 3.1 to illustrate a technical analysis.

After the price chart is complete, basic patterns are identified in the historical prices. In the short-term, prices can exhibit four basic patterns: stable, trend, seasonal, and shift. A stable pattern is essentially a horizontal line with little movement up or down. A trend shows upward or downward price movements. Seasonal patterns are repeating patterns occurring over time. For example, gasoline prices in the United States typically increase during the summer vacation season. Seasonal patterns may be caused by actual seasonal changes, such as harvesting for an agricultural commodity or changes in consumer demand. A shift is a step change occurring—for example—after a major disruption to supply or demand.

Table 3.1 Natural gas: Citygate prices (US$/1,000 cubic ft.),
January 2014 to March 2016

Month	2014	2015	2016
January	$5.56	$4.48	$3.38
February	$6.41	$4.54	$3.46
March	$6.57	$4.35	$3.45
April	$5.64	$3.93	
May	$5.90	$4.24	
June	$6.05	$4.43	
July	$5.99	$4.65	
August	$5.49	$4.58	
September	$5.51	$4.54	
October	$5.16	$4.00	
November	$4.91	$3.68	
December	$5.15	$3.76	

Source: U.S. Energy Information Administration.[3]

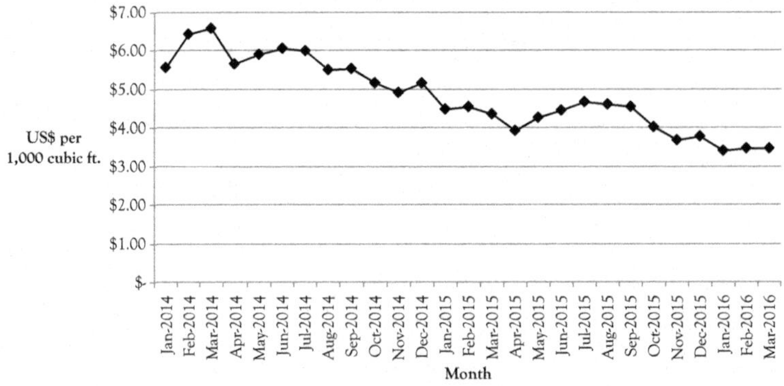

Figure 3.1 Natural gas: Citygate prices, January 2014 to March
2016

Source: U.S. Energy Information Administration.[4]

Besides the basic patterns, some prices may be a combination of patterns. For example, a seasonal pattern can also have an increasing or decreasing trend. In the long-term, a cyclical pattern from economic cycles may also be evident.

Random error is present in all pricing patterns. Over time price patterns change, and for some commodities, frequent changes can occur.

Determining price patterns is more of an art than a science and requires judgment and experience. Since all price patterns contain random error, it is difficult to sort out real changes in patterns from those that are noise. Note the monthly prices for natural gas are shown in Figure 3.1. Overall during this time period there had been a downward trend in price. However, during this period there were some months, for example, April through July 2015 when prices increased. Further, in February and March 2016, prices appear to have stabilized. There is no "right" answer to the patterns, as this depends on judgment, which is gained through experience. So when a trend is occurring, how far will prices increase or decrease? Patterns emerge because of market participants' beliefs and behaviors. Prices tend to increase or decrease until they hit upper and lower boundaries formed by the behaviors of the market participants. At the upper end is a resistance price that is the "highest" price for the commodity. When an upward trend encounters the resistance price, it typically shifts direction and begins to decline. Similarly, a low price point called support is the price that a decreasing trend typically reverses.

Commodity traders use short-term price charts with frequent intervals, often as short as 1 minute, to identify support and resistant points. For natural gas over the entire time period, as shown in Figure 3.1, the resistance price appears to be $6.57 per 1,000 cubic ft., and the support price is $3.45 per 1,000 cubic ft. The resistance and support prices can change over time. A shift in the pattern caused by a major supply disruption or economic jolt will shift the resistance and support prices.

In technical analysis, there are a number of standard price patterns beyond the scope of this book that experienced analysts use to identify trends and trend reversals. It takes time to study and learn about commodities and begin to develop an understanding of their normal pricing patterns. Understanding pricing patterns provides critical information for making better commodity management decisions.

Selecting a Forecasting Model

Commodity traders use a wide variety of technical analysis tools to understand very short-term pricing patterns, so they can profit from price movements. Supply chain managers, whose objective is to understand commodity price risk and buy to budget, can use a subset of these tools. Some statistical tools useful for short-term forecasting for supply chain management include time-series models, simple linear regression, and seasonal indices. If you did not know anything about forecasting, how would you develop a short-term forecast? One simple approach is to take the last period's price and use it as a forecast for the next period's price, an approach called the naïve method. For example, using the data in Table 3.1, the actual price in March 2016 of $3.45/1,000 cubic ft. would be the forecast for April 2016. Once the actual price for April 2016 is known, that price becomes the forecast for May 2016. Although this approach is easy, the forecast may not be very accurate since it may introduce a lot of random noise.

Some simple statistical tools can be used to improve forecasts. Different statistical tools are designed for different pricing patterns: stable prices, increasing or decreasing trends, seasonal patterns, and a combination of trend and seasonality. The price pattern determines which statistical tool is likely to work the best. For example, if the price pattern is actually an upward trend, but the forecast is developed using a statistical tool designed for a stable pattern, the forecast will be too low.

Developing Forecasts for Stable Price Patterns

Three statistical tools called time-series models are designed for stable price patterns. These statistical tools are simple moving average, weighted moving average, and simple exponential smoothing. With spreadsheets these tools are easy to develop and use.

The easiest model to use is the simple moving average. A simple moving average is the average price over a fixed number of time periods, for example, months. Look back at the monthly price data for natural gas in Table 3.1. To examine this model, take for example a three-month moving average to forecast the price of natural gas beginning in April 2014. To develop the forecast, average the prices for January ($5.56/1,000 cubic ft.), February ($6.41/1,000 cubic ft.), and March ($6.57/1,000 cubic ft.). The three-month moving average forecast for April is $6.18/1,000 cubic ft. Once the actual price is known for April ($5.64/1,000 cubic ft.), a three-month moving average forecast can be developed for May 2014

($6.21/1,000 cubic ft.) by averaging the prices for February, March, and April. Then, the forecast for June 2014 can be developed by averaging the prices for March, April, and May. Continue this approach to develop a price forecast for each subsequent month. Typically, three to six time periods are used for simple moving averages. When fewer time periods are used, the forecasts are more responsive to recent price changes. Using more time periods creates a smoothing effect, so the forecast has less variation and is more stable. For example, Figure 3.2 compares forecasts for natural gas. The solid line is the actual spot price for natural gas; the dotted line is the three-month moving average forecast, and the dashed line is the six-month moving average forecast. The six-month moving average has less variance and is more stable than the three-month moving average. Later in this chapter, we will discuss how to measure the accuracy of a forecasting model, so the models can be compared and the best model can be selected.

The weighted moving average also is intuitive and easy to use. With the simple moving average, to improve forecast accuracy the only factor to adjust is the number of periods averaged together. With the weighted moving average, there are two factors to improve accuracy: the number of periods and the weight put on the price in each period.

As a first step, similar to the simple moving average model, select the number of periods to include in the model, which is typically three to six

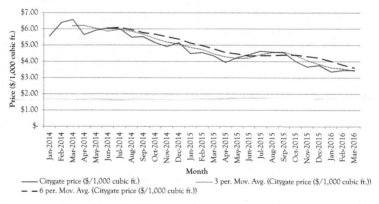

Figure 3.2 Natural gas: Three- and six-month simple moving average forecasts

Source: U.S. Department of Energy.[5]

periods. Then, based on judgment, assign a weight to each time period so the weights sum to one. The most recent time period typically reflects future prices more accurately than older time periods. Thus the price for the most recent time period is usually weighted the most heavily. The final step of the weighted moving average model is to add the weighted prices for each time period together to get the forecast for the next period.

For example, we will forecast the price of natural gas for April 2014 using a three-month weighted moving average. Using judgment, decide on the weights to use. In this case, weigh the most recent month (March) at 0.5; the next most recent month (February) is weighted at 0.3; and the oldest month (January) is weighted at 0.2. The calculations are shown in Table 3.2. Using a three-month weighted moving average, the forecast for April 2014 is $6.32/1,000 cubic ft.

Once the actual price for April is known ($5.64/1,000 cubic ft.), the forecast for May is calculated by 0.2 × February price ($6.41/1,000 cubic ft.), 0.3 × March price ($6.57/1,000 cubic ft.), and 0.5 × April price ($5.64/1,000 cubic ft.). Using the three-month weighted moving average, the forecast for May 2014 is $6.07/1,000 cubic ft. The process continues as the actual price for each new month is known.

Another model designed for stable price patterns is simple exponential smoothing. This model determines the forecast for the next period using the actual price and forecast for the last period. Thus, the forecast for the price in April 2014 is based on the actual price in March 2014 and the price forecast for March 2014.

Only one factor is adjusted in the simple exponential smoothing model. This factor refers to a smoothing coefficient, and is named α.

Table 3.2 Natural gas: Three-month weighted moving average forecast April 2014

Month	Price (US$/1,000 cubic ft.)	Weight	Weighted price
January	$5.56	0.2	$1.11
February	$6.41	0.3	$1.92
March	$6.57	0.5	$3.29
April	Forecast = Sum	1	$6.32

Source: U.S. Energy Information Administration.[6]

Using judgment, a value should be assigned to α between 0 and 1. The actual price in the last period is multiplied by α, and the forecast for the last period is weighted by $(1 - \alpha)$. A higher value of α puts more weight on the actual price.

These two values are added together to get the forecast for the next period. To put more weight on the most recent price, use a high value for α.

The equation for simple exponential smoothing is as follows:

$$\text{Forecast (period } t + 1) = \alpha \times \text{Price (period } t) + (1 - \alpha)$$
$$\times \text{Forecast (period } t)$$

A starting forecast is required to begin a simple exponential model. One approach is to use the actual price for the last period as an estimate for a forecast to get started. To develop a forecast for April 2014, you need both the actual price and a forecast for March 2014. For example, the actual price for March 2014 is $6.57/1,000 cubic ft. However, there is no forecast for March 2014. As an estimate, use the actual price for February 2014 as the forecast for March. If you use a value of 0.8, the forecast for April is as follows:

$$\text{Forecast (April 2014)} = 0.8 \times \text{Price (March 2014)} + (1 - 0.8)$$
$$\times \text{Forecast (March 2014)}$$

$$\$6.54/1{,}000 \text{ cubic ft.} = (0.8 \times \$6.57/1{,}000 \text{ cubic ft.})$$
$$+ (0.2 \times \$6.41/1{,}000 \text{ cubic ft.}).$$

After the actual price for April 2014 is known, a forecast for May 2014 is developed. Now there is an actual price for April ($5.64/1,000 cubic ft.) and a forecast for April ($6.54/1,000 cubic ft.). The forecast for May is as follows:

$$\text{Forecast (May 2014)} = 0.8 \times \text{Price (April 2014)} + (1 - 0.8)$$
$$\times \text{Forecast (April 2014)}$$

$$\$5.82/1{,}000 \text{ cubic ft.} = (0.8 \times \$5.64/1{,}000 \text{ cubic ft.})$$
$$+ (0.2 \times \$6.54/1{,}000 \text{ cubic ft.}).$$

After the model is developed, it is continually applied to forecast each subsequent month. Over time, any error introduced by the initial forecast's estimate will diminish. The key to developing a good simple exponential smoothing forecasting model is to select a value of α having the highest forecast accuracy. As we will explain later in the chapter, you can compare different values of α to determine which value results in the most accurate forecast.

One of the major limitations of the three time-series models is they only forecast one period ahead. Although they are helpful to support short-term tactical decisions, the limited visibility is problematic for strategic decisions.

Developing Forecasts for Price Patterns with Trends

The three statistical tools illustrated so far all work well for short-term forecasts when the price pattern is relatively stable. However, in many cases, historical prices are increasing or decreasing. If prices are increasing, the forecasts developed using time-series models for a stable pattern underestimate prices. If prices are decreasing, models for stable patterns will overestimate prices. There is an extension of the exponential smoothing model called trend-adjusted exponential smoothing that can be used for trend patterns. Please refer to a comprehensive textbook on business forecasting for more detailed information about these models.

Another easy method, simple linear regression, can be used for short-term forecasts with stable or trend-price patterns. Also called "least-squared," this model mathematically fits a line to the price data points, so the sum of the squared distance from each point to the line is minimized. Linear regression models can be easily calculated using an Excel spreadsheet. One approach is to create a scatter chart replacing the months with the number in the time-series sequence as shown in Figure 3.3 for natural gas prices. Using the layout tab in Excel, click on the data in the scatter chart and then insert a linear trend line. Be sure to select the option to show the equation and the R^2 on the chart.

The R^2 indicates how well the regression line fits the data. If there is a poor fit, the regression line should not be used as a forecasting tool. The R^2 value can range from 0 to 1 and shows the amount of variance in the

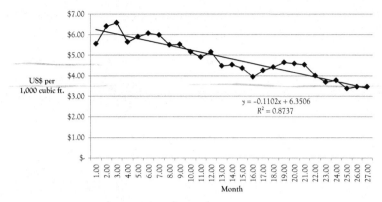

$$y = -0.1102x + 6.3506$$
$$R^2 = 0.8737$$

Figure 3.3 Natural gas: simple linear regression forecast

Source: U.S. Energy Information Administration.[7]

price data that is explained by the trend line. A value of 1 indicates a perfect fit of the trend line to the price data. In fact, if the R^2 is 1, the trend line would be exactly on top of all the price data points. With real price data a perfect fit is unlikely.

The simple linear regression for the natural gas price data is shown in Figure 3.3. The R^2 is a good fit of 0.87. This suggests that simple linear regression is a good forecasting tool to use for a commodity, since 87 percent of the variance in price is accounted for by the trend line. There is no rule of thumb of how high an R^2 should be to be acceptable, but the higher the R^2 the better. If the R^2 is acceptable, then the equation can be used to forecast price.

To develop the forecast for April 2014, you use the regression equation $y = -0.11x + 6.35$. In the equation, y is the forecast for the price of natural gas and x is the number corresponding to the month. As the chart started at January 2014, April 2014 is month 4, so the x value is 4. Solving the equation ($y = -0.11(4) + 6.35$) shows a price forecast of $5.91/1,000 cubic ft. for April 2014. You can use the regression equation to forecast the price in April 2016. The number for April 2016 is 28. Insert 28 as x and solve the equation. The forecast for April 2016 is $3.27/1,000 cubic ft.

One benefit of simple linear regression is it can be used for any number of periods into the future. As long as you expect prices to follow the same trend, the simple linear regression model should be a good fit.

This overcomes the limitation of the time-series models forecasting only one period ahead. However, when the price pattern changes, for example, when resistance or support prices are encountered, the regression developed is no longer appropriate and will not provide an accurate forecast. A forecasting model must be developed fitting the new price pattern. For example, if natural gas prices stabilize and begin to increase in the summer of 2016, you would need to develop new model reflecting the new increasing price trend.

Developing Forecasts for Seasonal Price Patterns

Statistical tools can also be used to develop forecasts if commodity prices show seasonal patterns. A seasonal pattern consistently repeats itself over time. A seasonal model should be used if seasonality in commodity prices is observed. At least two years of data are needed to determine if there are monthly or quarterly seasonal patterns.

Review the quarterly price data for two years shown in Table 3.3. Note that Quarter 5 in the table is the first quarter of the second year. There seems to be a repeating pattern in the first and second years. In each year, the highest prices are in the last quarter, with the next to highest being in the first quarter. If this type of pattern is expected to continue, a seasonal forecasting model should be used. To develop seasonal indices, the first step is to develop a regression equation to fit the data. This line

Table 3.3 Seasonal price indices

Quarter	Spot price US$/gallon	Trend-line price	Seasonal index	Average index
1	$1.61	$1.33	1.21	1.22
2	$1.35	$1.53	0.88	0.95
3	$1.24	$1.72	0.72	0.71
4	$2.10	$1.92	1.09	1.12
5	$2.61	$2.12	1.23	
6	$2.37	$2.32	1.02	
7	$1.76	$2.52	0.70	
8	$3.14	$2.71	1.16	

Source: U.S. Energy Information Administration.[8]

represents prices with seasonality removed. The R^2 will likely be low but is not a concern because the trend line itself is not generating the forecast.

For the data in Table 3.3, the regression equation is $y = 0.198x + 1.131$. Then calculate quarterly prices without seasonality by entering the number for each quarter as "x" in the regression equation. Develop a seasonal index for each time period by dividing the actual price in that time period by the trend-line price for that time period. In this example, the seasonal index for Quarter 1 (1.21) is the actual spot price ($1.61/gallon) divided by the regression line price ($1.33/gallon).

To develop final indices to be used for forecasting, average the indices for the same time period across at least two years. In the example, average the indices for Quarter 1 and Quarter 5 (first quarter in year 2) together to get the index used to forecast the first quarter of each year. Repeat for the remaining quarters. The average indices are used to generate the forecast.

Next, use the average seasonal indices to develop a forecast for Quarter 9, which is Quarter 1 of the third year. Return to the regression equation ($y = 0.198x + 1.131$) and enter 9 for x. This is the trend-line price of $2.91/gallon. Now multiply this price by 1.22, the seasonal index for Quarter 1. The forecast for the first quarter of the third year is $3.56/gallon. The forecast for Quarter 10, which is the second quarter of the third year, is determined by multiplying the trend-line price of $3.11 by the seasonal index for Quarter 2 (0.95). The forecast for the second quarter of the third year is $2.96.

Assessing Forecast Accuracy

We have examined a number of different forecasting methods in this chapter. Developing and maintaining commodity price forecasts consume time and money, so use the simplest method providing the accuracy needed for the decisions being made. If the consequences of an error are larger, the forecast accuracy should be better.

Forecast error is the key measure of forecast accuracy. The actual price minus the forecast price for a period is its forecast error. An example is shown using a subset of the historical data for natural gas from January 2014 to December 2014 shown in Table 3.4 to compare forecasts with

Table 3.4 Forecast error for three- and six-month moving average forecasts

Month	Citygate price ($/1,000 cubic ft.)	Three-month MA	Three-month error	Six-month MA	Six-month error
Jan 2014	$5.56				
Feb 2014	$6.41				
Mar 2014	$6.57				
Apr 2014	$5.64	$6.18	$(0.54)		
May 2014	$5.90	$6.21	$(0.31)		
Jun 2014	$6.05	$6.04	$0.01		
Jul 2014	$5.99	$5.86	$0.13	$6.02	$(0.03)
Aug 2014	$5.49	$5.98	$(0.49)	$6.09	$(0.60)
Sep 2014	$5.51	$5.84	$(0.33)	$5.94	$(0.43)
Oct 2014	$5.16	$5.66	$(0.50)	$5.76	$(0.60)
Nov 2014	$4.91	$5.39	$(0.48)	$5.68	$(0.77)
Dec 2014	$5.15	$5.19	$(0.04)	$5.52	$(0.37)

Source: U.S. Energy Information Administration.[9]

three- and six-month simple moving average models. Although the three-month moving average starts April 2014, July 2014 is the first forecast that can be developed using the six-month simple moving average because data from January to June are needed.

For example, the actual price for July 2014 is $5.99/1,000 cubic ft. The three-month simple moving average forecast for July 2014 is $5.86/1,000 cubic ft., so the forecast error (price minus forecast) for July is $0.13. The six-month simple moving average forecast for July 2014 is $6.02, so the forecast error is −$0.03.

As shown in Table 3.4, it is difficult to compare the accuracy of forecasting methods by looking at the individual forecast errors period by period. Several metrics make it easier to compare forecasting methods. These are the mean forecast error (MFE), the mean absolute deviation (MAD), and the mean absolute percent error (MAPE).

The MFE is simply the average of the forecast errors over the time periods evaluated. It is a measure of the bias of a forecast. A positive MFE value shows that the forecasts are, on average, too low. On average, the actual price is greater than the forecast price. When the MFE is negative, the forecast tends to be too high relative to the actual price. In the natural gas example for 2014, the three-month simple moving average for natural gas has an MFE of −$2.55 while the six-month forecast has an MFE of −$2.81. Both models overestimate the price, with the three-month model being slightly less biased than the six-month model. Given that the pattern shows a downward trend, forecasting models designed for stable patterns would be expected to overestimate the price. More advanced forecasting models such as trend-adjusted exponential smoothing is specifically designed for a trend should provide a more accurate forecast. To learn more about this method, we suggest consulting a basic statistical text book or the Internet.

A problem with the MFE is high positive and high negative forecast errors can cancel each other out, resulting in a low MFE but poor forecasts. The second metric, MAD, addresses this problem. The MAD is the average of the absolute values of the forecast errors; thus, it reflects the true size of the error better than MFE. The MAD for three- and six-month simple moving average models, respectively, are $0.31 and $0.47, suggesting the three-month moving average is a better method. Given the downward price trend, you would expect a model with fewer periods would be more accurate.

The MAPE is the average of the absolute value error as a percent of the actual price for each time period. In the example, the three-month moving average has a MAPE of 5.8 percent, and the six-month moving average's value is 8.6 percent. The MFE, MAD, and MAPE suggest the three-month moving average provide a more accurate forecast than the six-month moving average. However, a model specifically incorporating a trend is likely to be even more accurate.

Improving the Forecast

If the values of MFE, MAD, and MAPE suggest the accuracy of the forecast is not acceptable, then additional work must be done. The first step is to adjust parameters with the current model. For example, in the simple moving average model, this would involve increasing or decreasing the number of periods. In the weighted moving average, the weights can be changed, the number of periods, or both. In the simple exponential smoothing model, adjust the values. If adjusting the parameters of the current model does not improve the forecast, a different model can be applied and parameters adjusted until an acceptable forecast is developed.

Developing effective and reliable forecasts requires investing in appropriate organizational resources. You should not strive to develop a perfect forecast, because no matter how good the forecast is, it will contain error. Instead, enough resources should be devoted to develop a forecast that is accurate enough for your organization's decision-making needs.

Monitoring the Forecast

Once a good forecasting model has been identified, then it should be applied to generate a forecast. Before using this forecast to make decisions, adjust it if necessary based on judgment and experience. The biggest challenge with technical analysis is assessing if the price pattern will continue or change. Understanding market fundamentals, which will be described in Chapter 4, provides information that should be integrated with the technical forecast, using judgment to make the final forecast.

It is important to monitor the forecast's performance over time and adjust the forecast if needed. Pricing patterns can quickly change, so it is necessary to continuously track a forecast's performance. To monitor a forecast's performance over time, a metric called "tracking signal" can be used. The tracking signal is the ratio of the running sum of the forecast errors divided by the MAD.[10] Calculate a tracking signal for each period and compare it to control limits determined by ±3 MAD. A point outside the control limits suggests the forecasting model should be reevaluated.

Summary

This chapter describes how to use technical analysis to develop short-term forecasts. Technical analysis relies solely on historical price patterns that in the short-term can be stable, trend, seasonal, or a combination of these patterns. The appropriate statistical tools to use for developing the forecast depend on the price patterns. Time-series models—such as simple moving averages, weighted moving averages, and simple exponential smoothing—are designed for stable price patterns. When trends exist, forecasts can be developed using more complex time-series models or simple linear regression. Season indices are used to develop forecasts when prices have seasonal patterns.

Select the forecast model and parameters providing the accuracy needed by examining forecast error. Simple metrics, such as MFE, MAD, and MAPE, use forecast error to indicate a forecast's accuracy. Use judgment and experience to adjust technical forecasts before using them to support decisions. Monitor ongoing forecasting performance, which can rapidly change as pricing patterns frequently shift.

CHAPTER 4

Forecasting Long-Term Commodity Prices

When long-term forecasts are needed, technical analysis methods based on price patterns alone are not adequate. This is because, in the long run, too many factors impact the price of the commodity, thereby changing its pattern. Further, you cannot depend on historical pricing patterns to continue far into the future because the factors affecting the value of the commodity can quickly change. Instead, forecasters examine the underlying factors affecting supply and demand and use their judgment to forecast price. This approach is called fundamental analysis.

In this chapter, we explain how to develop long-term forecasts for different types of commodities using fundamental analysis. In fundamental analysis, the underlying assumption is the balance between a commodity's supply and its demand establishes its price. Fundamental analysis uses qualitative reasoning to understand supply and demand, along with statistical approaches, but ultimately it depends on judgment to forecast price.

There are eight key steps in the fundamental analysis process. The first step is to gather information on supply, demand, and price. This step involves plotting supply, demand, and price data and looking at their relationships. The next step consists of building an understanding of the basics of supply—learning the underlying factors affecting supply and estimating how supply may change in the future. Similarly, this step requires an analysis and understanding of the basics of demand—of the underlying factors affecting demand and of how demand may change in the future. After applying reasoning to qualitatively assess supply and demand, the relationships between supply, demand, and price are examined using statistical tools. The correlation evaluates the strength and direction of relationships with price. If the correlation is significant, a model to estimate price can be developed using simple linear regression. If there is a financial market for the commodity, the next step incorporates future price trends qualitatively into the analysis. All the knowledge obtained about the commodity, prices from regression models, and futures prices will be combined to develop the final forecast, using judgment.

This chapter explains each of the following steps of the fundamental analysis process:

1. Gathering information.
2. Understanding supply basics.
3. Identifying underlying factors affecting supply.
4. Understanding demand basics.
5. Identifying underlying factors affecting demand.
6. Examining correlations and developing regression models.
7. Considering future prices.
8. Developing and monitoring the final forecast.

Gathering Information

Finding specific supply, demand, and price data is one of the biggest challenges with a fundamental analysis. For some commodities, data is publicly available, but for others, that is not the case. For many traditional commodities, the U.S. government can be a source of useful information from the United States and the world. The U.S. Department of Agriculture (USDA) Economic Research Service (crops and livestock), the U.S. Energy Information Administration (oil, coal, natural gas, and electricity), and the U.S. Geological Survey (metals and other minerals) websites are excellent sources of information about supply, demand, and prices for many commodities. Some of these government agencies also publish their own forecasts. For example, the USDA publishes reports of supply and demand forecasts for agricultural commodities for a 10-year period, which is available on the USDA website.[1] Industrial associations such as the International Cocoa Association, the International Coffee Organization, and the Aluminum Association are also sources of commodity information and statistics.

Table 4.1 provides a summary of some information sources and categories you can use to identify factors influencing supply and demand, such as global events and economic trends, industrial and technological changes, supplier and customer behaviors, and governmental policies. Often it is not just one event or change in the market, but rather it is the interaction of numerous conditions influencing commodity prices.

It can be difficult to find the exact data needed for a fundamental analysis, depending on the commodity. Further, having timely access to new information is especially critical. The market quickly adjusts so new information can dramatically change a forecast. Thus, if your organization does not have the internal resources to devote to doing commodity research, consider using a subscription service providing analysis from experts who focus on understanding specific commodities. Considering the internal resources needed for finding and analyzing data, the benefit of a subscription service may outweigh its costs. However, it is important to stay knowledgeable about the commodity in order to use the information provided by the subscription service to make good supply chain decisions.

Table 4.1 Market intelligence sources[2]

Type of resource	Examples			
Company financial research	Securities and Exchange Commission (SEC) filings (Edgar online)	Fortune 500	Annual reports	
Global business references	Supplier directories	Embassies and consulates	Harvard Business School	U.S. Department of Commerce
Industry links	North American Industry Classification System (NAIS); Standard Industrial Classification (SIC)	Sematech	Raw material indexes	United Nations Standard Products and Services Code (UNSPSC)
Commodity and labor statistics	U.S. Bureau of Labor Statistics (BLS)	U.S. Department of Agriculture (USDA)	U.S. Energy Information Administration (EIA)	U.S. Geological Survey (USGS)
Economic indicators	Central Intelligence Agency Factbook	Worldtrade Organization (WtO)	World Bank	OANDA

A starting point in understanding a commodity is to visually assess the relationships among supply, demand, and price. This step consists of gathering annual supply, demand, and price data for 10 to 20 years. A commodity's total supply includes its new production, recycled materials if applicable, and its stocks. Stocks are the amount of a commodity stored in inventory. Stocks can be held by any supply chain member, such as producers, distributors, and end users.

Governments also can hold stocks; for example, the U.S. Strategic Petroleum Reserve holds oil in inventory. Imports should be included if the analysis is focused on supply within a specific country rather than on worldwide supply. For some commodities, demand is called consumption. Demand can be examined on a worldwide basis or country-by-country, in which case exports of that country should be included as one component of demand.

After gathering data, annual data are plotted for supply, demand, and price for the commodity on the same line graph. Show supply and demand on the primary vertical *y*-axis on the left and show price on the secondary vertical *y*-axis on the right. Analyze the graph, looking for patterns, relationships, and unusual shifts. Typically, price increases when the surplus of supply relative to demand decreases. As the surplus of supply relative to demand increases, price typically decreases. Are there spikes, drops, or shifts in patterns? Researching the history of the commodity is important for understanding why these changes in supply, demand, and price have occurred.

Let's take a look at an example. Figure 4.1 shows U.S. supply, demand, and price for natural gas from 2000 to 2015.[3] From 2000 to 2004 the levels of supply and demand were very close to each other. The price decrease in 2002 at an average of $2.95 per cubic ft. is attributed to an economic slowdown beginning in 2001 and continued through much of 2002. The economic recovery that followed drove natural gas prices higher.

In 2005, when hydraulic fracking technology enabled the extraction of natural gas trapped in shale rock to become economically viable, natural gas supply increased, increasing the surplus of supply over demand. However, also in 2005, two major hurricanes caused production shutdowns in the Gulf of Mexico leading to a high spike in price to $7.33 per cubic ft. in late 2005. The dramatic price drop in 2008 and 2009

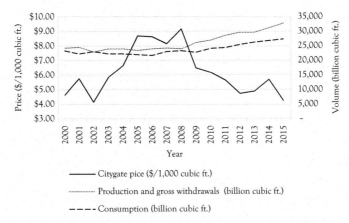

Figure 4.1 U.S. natural gas supply, demand, and price, 2000 to 2015

Source: U.S. Energy Information Administration.[4]

is attributed to a decline in industrial demand because of a major recession. As supply from shale gas production continued to outpace demand from 2009 onward prices have continued to decline. One exception is the spike in price in 2014, which is attributed to cold winter weather because natural gas is used for heating. Once you have good understanding of the overview of supply, demand, and price for the commodity, the next step in a fundamental analysis is to learn more about the underlying factors driving supply and demand. This knowledge is used to estimate the change in supply and the change in demand during the future time period needed for forecasting.

Understanding Supply Basics

This step begins with focusing on a commodity's supply market. Who are the participants in the commodity's supply network and what are their roles? Depending on the commodity there may be many tiers in a commodity's supply network. The natural gas supply network consists of producers who extract natural gas using traditional wells or from shale rock; processors who remove water and impurities to convert natural gas so it is ready for use; and pipeline operators who transport natural gas from production to users, storage operators, marketers, and local distributors. Some supply networks may have vertically integrated members who own different parts of the network and perform more than one of the key supply functions.

A bottleneck restricting capacity of any one of the key functions in a commodity's supply network will reduce its supply. The commodity's supply will be limited by the part of its supply network having the lowest capacity; therefore, there is a need to identify which aspect of the supply network may represent a bottleneck. For example, with natural gas, bottlenecks could be caused by the number of gas wells, the capacity of pipelines used to transport gas, or the capacity of underground caverns used to store natural gas. When capacity is expanded at the bottleneck function, then the bottleneck shifts to another part of the supply network.

Further, understanding the basics of supply requires learning about how, where, and when the commodity is produced now and how production may change in the future. Several different production methods are used for some commodities, and new technologies can lead to new production methods. Typically, different production methods have different cost structures. As commodity prices increase or new production technology is developed, some production methods previously not economical become viable and can open new sources of supply. For example, natural gas was traditionally produced by drilling a vertical well for the gas to flow upward. Historically, natural gas production was determined by the number of wells. Since the mid-2000s, advances in hydraulic fracking have changed natural gas production dramatically increasing supply.[5]

The number of entities producing the commodity should be considered in a fundamental analysis. When there are many producers, each respective entity makes independent decisions about how much to produce based on estimated profit, considering the commodity's expected selling price. In this situation, no single market participant has a significant influence on supply and ultimately price. Traditionally, agricultural products were in this situation since many farmers were independent operators of family farms. For some mineral commodities, because of the high cost of mining, a few firms may own the production capacity and thus can have a significant influence on supply and price.

For agricultural commodities, the potential number of acres and the characteristics of the actual crop yield affect production. Individual farmers make decisions about how many acres to plant of different crops based on profit potential. So, if in a given year, the price of a crop increases because it is in short supply, the next year farmers are likely to plant more acres, thereby increasing supply and driving down prices. In general, in developed countries, crop yield has increased significantly and continues to increase because of advances in seed, fertilizer, equipment, and technology, for example Global Positioning System (GPS). A higher yield per acre increases production.

For some metals—such as steel, copper, and aluminum—recycling from scrap, referred to as the secondary market, is an important consideration in supply. Thus, there is a need for understanding how primary markets for new production, as well as secondary markets for scrap, affect supply and, in turn, prices. As commodity prices increase, recycling can become a viable alternative to new production. For example, in the United States, recycled aluminum often exceeds new primary-market production.[6] Recycled aluminum includes waste from manufacturing processes as well as aluminum used in products and returned from consumers, such as aluminum cans.

In the long run, recycling is likely to increase as the world's demand for minerals and metals increases. Higher commodity prices make it more economical to invest in technologies for recycling. For example, historically, very little lithium was recycled. With the growth of lithium batteries in electronics and the projected growth for hybrid and electric cars, recycled lithium will be more competitively priced, and the market for recycled lithium is likely to increase.[7]

Location is also an important factor to consider. Production and transportation costs are often influenced by a commodity's production location. For example, most natural gas produced in the United States is also consumed there and thus can be transported by pipeline. However, using liquid natural gas (LNG) technology, negative 260 degrees, opening up new sources of natural gas, such as Trinidad and Tobago, which were not feasible using conventional methods.[8] However, with the economic and technical feasibility of shale gas, there is less focus on using LNG technology to import natural gas into the United States. Instead, LNG technology may be used for exports from the United States.

Globalization has a significant impact on supply. In the past, when agricultural commodities such as corn and soybeans were primarily produced and consumed in the same region, supply would greatly increase at harvest time and then steadily decrease throughout the year. However, many food crops are produced in both the northern and southern hemispheres. Global trade and economic ocean transport reduce the impact of the harvest season in any one region on supply and price. For example, corn is typically planted in the United States during April and May and harvested in October and November. In Brazil, the planting season ranges from October to December and harvesting from February until June, and some areas of Brazil can do two plantings a year.[9]

Some commodities are produced in many regions of the world while others may be limited to a specific region, depending on natural resources or climate required. When production is concentrated in a few regions, the risk of a supply disruption increases. Cocoa, for example, can only be grown in rainforest conditions occurring plus or minus 10 degrees of the equator, limiting production to a few countries. In fact, over 30 percent of the world's cocoa is grown in a single country, Côte d'Ivoire, which has a history of political instability increasing the risk of a disruption of cocoa supply.[10] In another example, Chile has over 50 percent of the world's known lithium reserves, and thus the shift to hybrid and electric vehicles will leave the world dependent on this South American country.[11]

Organization of the Petroleum Exporting Countries (OPEC) is perhaps the best-known example of how a coalition of countries attempts to influence supply and price. OPEC, with its 12 member countries, has about a 40 percent market share of the world's conventional oil supply and 60 percent of global oil trade.[12] The members of OPEC meet to discuss and agree upon production quotas for oil, which impacts price. However, the differing political agendas of the member countries means reaching agreement is difficult. Further, some members do not comply with production quotas, reducing the effectiveness of the agreements.

A commodity's stock levels, and the amount held in inventory, are part of supply. A commodity's inventory can be held across the supply network by a number of different market participants—including producers, consumers, commodity exchanges, and governments. Commodities with seasonal harvesting patterns are typically stored, with high stock levels, immediately after harvest, and the stock levels decline with use until the next harvest. Similarly, commodities with seasonal consumption also show seasonal stock patterns. For example, demand for fuel oil and natural gas in the United States is higher in the winter because of their use for heating. During the summer, natural gas is stored in underground caverns. In the winter, natural gas is withdrawn and used as a fuel for heating.

Long-term price is also influenced by proven or anticipated reserves for commodities such as oil, natural gas, minerals, and metals. Proven reserves are those extracted using known technology. For example, OPEC claims to have almost 80 percent of the world's proven conventional oil reserves.[13] New technology can lead to discoveries of new reserves of a commodity. For example, from 2010 to 2014, the U.S. Energy Information Administration estimates of recoverable natural gas from shale increased by over 100 percent.[14] However, a commodity's proven reserves do not necessarily lead to a future increase in actual supply.

Identifying Underlying Factors Affecting Supply

After examining the basics of supply for the commodity, all the underlying factors affecting supply in the future need to be identified, as well as the extent to which you expect supply to change because of these factors. Many factors can affect a commodity's supply including weather and climate, new technology, prices of other commodities, government policies and regulations, political instability, and input prices. Different underlying factors influence different commodities. In this section, we will discuss each of the major categories of underlying factors.

The time frame over which the factor may have an influence on supply needs to be identified for each factor. Some factors may affect supply in the short-term while others may affect supply in the long-term. Next, the impact of each factor upon supply is estimated by examining historical events and their impact on supply in the past—as well as how industry experts expect supply to change in the future.

Weather is a major factor affecting the supply of many commodities, especially agricultural crops. For crops such as corn, wheat, soybeans, and cotton, too much rain or flooding during the planting season means fewer acres can be planted, thereby reducing production. Even if a crop is successfully planted during the growing season, too much or too little rain is a problem, reducing crop yield. Of course, the weather at harvest time can also impact crop yield. In some extreme situations crops planted cannot be harvested because of the weather. In contrast, when the weather is favorable, production of agricultural commodities can exceed expectations, thereby increasing supply.

Agricultural crops are not the only types of commodities whose supply can be affected by weather. Oil and natural gas production in the Gulf of Mexico is disrupted by the weather. When major hurricanes occur, for employee safety, production platforms must shut down, reducing supply. Damage to rigs, pipelines, and refineries can halt production for a significant amount of time, as was the case after Hurricanes Katrina and Rita in 2005. Severe weather also can disrupt mining operations.

It is impossible to correctly predict in advance the impact any single weather event will have on the supply of a commodity. However, it is important to understand the climate in which commodities are produced. For example, it is probable during any hurricane season that oil and natural gas production in the Gulf of Mexico may be temporarily curtailed. In some years the chance is greater than others. The National Oceanic and Atmospheric Administration (NOAA; www.noaa.gov) is an excellent source of weather information such as drought and hurricane predictions. In fact, weather may pose a major challenge for commodity forecasting in the future. Scientists at NOAA suggest that in the United States, climate extremes have been increasing since the 1970s, and this phenomenon would be expected globally as well.[15] More extreme events, such as intense storms or very high or low temperatures, means weather is likely to have a greater impact on commodity production. Factors can also be related with each other, impacting on commodity price volatility. Starting in 2007, for example, durum wheat volatility increased significantly due to unfavorable weather conditions on all the continents, the related reduction of worldwide stock levels, and trader speculation in the financial markets. Some of the companies we involved in our studies highlighted that weather risk significantly affects price volatility, but this influence is difficult to manage, due to many other factors.

Incremental improvements in technology have a major impact on a commodity's supply over time. For example, advances in seed, fertilizer, irrigation methods, equipment, and farming practices have significantly improved crop yield for agricultural commodities. To illustrate this example, in the United States, corn yields have increased from 118 bushels per acre in 1990 to 168 bushels per acre in 2016.[16] More radical changes in technology, such as deep-water drilling for oil and the ability to extract natural gas from shale, can have a major impact on supply.

Commodity prices also determine how much of a commodity will be produced. As a commodity's price increases, there is more incentive for current producers to increase production levels and for new producers to enter the market. Of course as supply increases, if demand does not likewise increase, prices drop and over time production will also be reduced. In agricultural markets, farmers have the flexibility to shift between different crops, depending on which one they believe will bring the highest prices. Farmers face a high level of price risk and uncertainty because of unfavorable weather and thus seek to maximize their profits. For example, crops such as corn, soybeans, wheat, and cotton can be planted depending on expected prices. In another example, oil prices determine if it is economical to produce alternative liquid fuels such as biodiesel and ethanol, driving up prices for fuel crops such as soybeans and corn. Higher prices entice farmers to plant more of these crops, which when harvested, increase supply.

A producer's decision of how much of a commodity to produce is also affected by the availability and cost of its inputs such as labor, equipment, and materials. The cost of seed and fertilizer may cause a farmer to switch to an alternative crop. Since Brazil is the world's largest exporter of sugar, the world price of sugar is heavily influenced by their cost of production. As the cost of production increases, so does the cost of worldwide sugar.[17] Globalization and the search for lower cost inputs such as labor and energy are likely to shift commodity production to low-cost countries when possible. Governments use subsidies and tariffs to retain local production.

The cost and time required to add production capacity also influence supply. Grain crops are typically planted once per year, so once the planting decision is made it cannot be changed until the next year. For some commodities it can take years to add capacity. After planting, it takes coffee trees 3 to 4 years to bear fruit. Oil refineries and mines can take years of planning, approval, and construction before being operational.

Government regulations including environment, safety, energy usage, subsidies, and taxes can have a major effect on supply. The specific type of impact depends on the type of commodity. Government regulation or deregulation can impact the industry's structure and the number of market participants. Regulations can also impact the time required to develop new production or delivery capacity. Some industries such as mining, natural gas, and oil face an extensive government approval process, delaying capacity additions.

With globalization, many different governments with different policies and regulations can impact supply in different ways. For example, air pollution laws taking effect in 2016 in China are likely to influence the supply of primary aluminum production.[18] Another example is the Russian government's decision not to export grain in 2010 because of a severe drought, which resulted in higher worldwide wheat prices.[19]

Government subsidies can have a major impact on commodity supply. Sugar is perhaps the most heavily subsidized commodity in the world with most countries, including the United States, having some type of sugar subsidy.[20] Restricting supply through production quotas and import restrictions results in significantly higher prices for sugar in the United States than in the rest of the world.

Political instability and war can reduce a commodity's supply. For example, over the last 25 years, war and political instability in the Middle East have caused periodic oil disruptions and price spikes. Besides the actual supply disruption, political instability and war increase uncertainty of future supply, typically driving up prices.

A commodity's supply is likely to be affected in different ways by a number of these different factors. Some of them are internal to the organization or supply chain, while others are external, and are closely intertwined with the well-known PESTLE framework (Political, Economic, Social, Technological, Legal, and Environmental).

Some factors may increase supply while others may decrease supply. In doing a fundamental analysis, you need to consider the overall effect from all possible factors to determine the amount you believe supply will increase or decrease.

Let's take natural gas as an example. According to the Natural Gas Supply Association, underlying factors affecting the supply of natural gas in the United States are the availability of inputs (skilled workforce, equipment, and pipeline capacity), government regulations (permitting time and access to land), and weather.[21] However, since 2005, the number one factor affecting natural gas supply is the technology used to extract shale gas. In the long run, the U.S. Energy Information Administration projects natural gas production in the United States will increase steadily to a production rate in 2040 of over 35 trillion cubic ft. per year, a 46 percent increase over the production in 2012.[22]

In another example, assume you are developing a forecast for a commodity for three years from now. For the commodity assume you estimate new production technology will increase supply by 8 percent in 3 years. You estimate new government regulations will reduce supply by 3 percent. You believe other factors will not significantly impact supply in the next three years. Thus the most likely change in supply in 3 years is a 5 percent increase. If the current supply of the commodity is 100 million tons, the forecast supply in 3 years is 105 million tons.

Understanding Demand Basics

Once there is a good understanding of supply and the underlying factors affecting supply, the process is repeated for understanding the basics of demand. As with supply, U.S. government agencies track demand data for many commodities available free through websites. Other sources of demand data include industry associations and many data services charging a fee for data access. Often the term *consumption* is used to refer to demand.

To understand the basics of demand, key questions to ask are these: how is the commodity used; who uses the commodity; where is it being used; and what are technically viable substitutes, if any? Has demand changed over time and if so why? For example, in 2015 in the United States, the largest use of natural gas was to generate electricity, followed by industrial, residential, commercial, and other uses as shown in Figure 4.2.

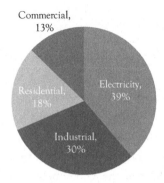

Figure 4.2 U.S. natural gas demand by sector, 2015

Source: U.S. Energy Information Administration.[23]

Examination of the major consumers of natural gas since 2001 shows residential and industrial use has declined slightly, while use of natural gas to generate electricity has increased typically replacing coal. Later in this chapter, we will discuss factors contributing to these changes.

To understand demand, it is important to understand where commodities are consumed. For example, because of rapid economic growth for years China's demand grew for many commodities driving up prices. However, by 2014, slowing growth softened demand and prices.[24]

Some commodities can be used for the same purpose and are often substituted based on price. Copper and aluminum can be used for the same purpose in many applications such as electronics and construction. Aluminum, titanium, and steel can be substituted for each other in some applications. High-fructose corn syrup and sugar can be substituted in many food products. Natural gas and coal can be substituted for each other in electricity generation. For your commodity, it is important to understand the technical challenges associated with using substitute commodities, as well as the effects that switching by competitors and firms in other industries may have on demand and, subsequently, on prices.

Identifying Underlying Factors Affecting Demand

Once there is a basic understanding of the factors affecting demand, all the underlying factors affecting demand in the future need to be identified as well as the extent to which demand may change because of these factors. In the long run, population growth, demographics, and economic development and growth affect demand. In addition, many factors affecting supply also affect demand. For example, weather and climate, prices of other commodities, government policies and regulations, new technologies, and customer tastes influence demand.

The world's population continues to grow resulting in increasing demand for commodities, especially in the areas of food, energy, and metals. The United Nations projects the world's population to grow from 7.3 billion in October 2015 to over 11 billion by 2100.[25] Populations are projected to grow the fastest in developing countries, especially in India and some countries in Africa. Over the long-term, the increased demand from population growth is likely to increase prices, especially for commodities such as oil and metals having limited reserves. Of course, demand for renewable commodities such as food and fiber also will increase with population growth.

While parts of the world that are growing will have younger populations, others will experience aging populations. Demographics affect demand for some commodities. For example, with aging populations, for health reasons, dietary patterns shift to reduce consumption of some commodities such as sugar.

Economic development and growth affect demand for commodities. In developing countries, as construction for homes, businesses, and infrastructure increases, so does the demand for commodities. Economic growth in manufacturing creates a need for commodity inputs. Economic growth and the development of a middle class increase demand for materials to produce consumer products. For example, demand for wool has increased because of demand from Chinese businessmen for tailored men's suits.[26]

Weather and climate affect demand for energy commodities. Harsh winters increase the demand for natural gas and fuel oil used for heating. Hot summers increase the demand for electricity and the commodities used to generate electricity such as natural gas and coal. A commodity's price can affect demand. As prices rise, consumers look for ways to use less of the commodity. When gasoline prices rise above a certain level, consumers drive less and purchase more fuel-efficient vehicles. If, as prices increase, there is a major drop in demand, economists say there is high price elasticity. If consumers still need the commodity and don't have a viable alternative, then demand may stay strong even if prices are high. This would be an example of an inelastic price.

For some commodities, consumers can switch to a different commodity used for the same purposes. If technically possible, consumers will use the commodity with the lowest price. As demand increases for that commodity, then its price increases relative to the other commodity and customers will switch back. Electrical power plants often have the capability to switch between the fuels of coal, oil, and natural gas, depending on price. In pipes and tubing, copper or plastic can be used. Depending on the prices, builders switch between products made from these commodities. Clothing can be made of cotton, plastic synthetic fibers such as acrylic, wool, or a blend of natural and synthetic fibers. Fabric manufacturers can shift depending on the prices of plastics or cotton, assuming customer tastes are accommodated. Soft drinks and processed foods can be formulated with sugar or high-fructose corn syrup.

The ease of switching and any costs involved with modifying the product or process must be considered when determining the price differential needed for substituting one commodity for another. For example, the fuel source (natural gas, fuel oil, or electricity) for residential and commercial buildings is normally fixed based on the heating system installed during construction. The heating system cannot be easily changed when fuel prices vary, so consumers cannot substitute fuel sources. Some processes used to manufacture plastics can use either natural gas or oil as a raw material. These processes can quickly and easily switch back and forth between raw materials depending on commodity prices. Historically, the ratio of the spot price of oil to the spot price of natural gas has been an indicator of when switching will occur. When the ratio becomes large enough it is economical for power generation and industrial uses to switch from using oil to using natural gas. In the long run, companies may redesign their products or processes to reduce the impact of substitution on customer perceptions or costs, as discussed in Chapter 5.

As with supply, government policies and regulations affect demand. The U.S. ethanol market is one influenced by subsidies in the form of tax breaks and tariffs and government mandates in terms of usage. In the United States, the government requires ethanol to be blended into gasoline. In turn, the ethanol market affects the demand for corn.

Technological advances can lead to increases or decreases in demand. For example, in pursuit of energy efficiency, advances in airplane design and manufacturing have increased the use of titanium in aerospace applications. Technology development in nonfood biofuels may lower demand for corn as a raw material for ethanol in the future. If successful in the long run, the demand for hybrid and electric cars is likely to reduce the demand for gasoline, but may increase the demand for electricity. In the long run, this might influence the demand for natural gas to generate electricity.

Changing customer tastes are a major factor affecting demand for some commodities. For example, in China where tea has been traditionally preferred over coffee, from 2014 to 2019, coffee consumption is expected to grow by 18 percent.[27] Demand for fiber commodities such as cotton and wool is affected by fashion trends. Food commodities are influenced by changes in dietary habits and fads. For example, lower wheat consumption in the United States has been attributed in part to the popularity of the low-carbohydrate diets in which dieters avoid breads and pastas.[28]

As was the case for supply, a commodity's demand is likely to be affected in different ways by a variety of factors, and some factors may increase demand while others may decrease demand. This requires assessing the positive and negative impacts from all relevant factors to forecast the change in demand for the future period of interest. Then, as illustrated with supply, current demand is adjusted upward or downward by the estimated percent change in demand to obtain the future level of demand.

Examining Correlations and Developing Regression Models

So far in this chapter we have described how to analyze and forecast underlying changes in a commodity's supply and demand. Commodity prices depend on the relationship between supply and demand as perceived by market participants. As supply increases relative to demand, prices tend to decrease. As supply decreases relative to demand, prices tend to increase. However, the market is always changing so when prices do increase, producers have more incentive to produce in larger quantities—and as a result, the gap between supply and demand widens, resulting in decreasing prices. The time frame in which these normal economic cycles occur differs by commodity.

A fundamental analysis uses qualitative judgments of the relationship between supply, demand, and price based on historical patterns to develop a forecast. For some commodities, the quantitative tools based on correlation and regression of historical data can provide useful information for decision making. We will analyze cotton data to demonstrate how to use correlation and regression for developing a long-term price forecast.

Return to the very first step in a fundamental analysis. One method for doing this is using a spreadsheet and plotting annual data for supply, demand, and price on a single-line graph as shown in Figure 4.3. Visually, it appears that as the gap between supply and demand narrows, cotton prices increase, and as the gap widens with more supply than demand, cotton prices decrease.

Let's create another graph making the relationship between supply, demand, and price easier to examine. In a spreadsheet, this involves subtracting total demand from total supply. This is the supply surplus. The supply surplus and price is plotted on a single-line graph with two vertical axes. For cotton this is shown in Figure 4.4. The graph shows, as would be expected, when the supply surplus increases, cotton prices decline, and when the supply surplus declines, prices increase. Thus for cotton, the

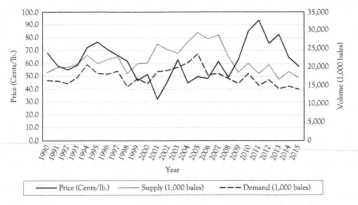

Figure 4.3 U.S. cotton supply, demand, and price, 1990 to 2015

Source: U.S. Department of Agriculture World Agricultural Supply and Demand Estimates (WASDE) Report on Cotton.[29]

Figure 4.4 U.S. cotton supply, surplus, and price, 1990 to 2015

Source: U.S. Department of Agriculture WASDE Report on Cotton.[30]

supply surplus and price appears to be negatively correlated as would be expected. If the correlation is reasonably strong, a regression equation can be used to forecast the price of cotton.

You can use a spreadsheet or statistical software to calculate a Pearson correlation coefficient (r), which shows the strength of the relationship between two variables. In this example, the variables are supply surplus and cotton price. The value of r is between −1 and 1. An r value of −1 means there is a perfect negative correlation between the variables, so the variables move perfectly in opposite directions to each other. An r value of 0 shows there is no relationship between the variables. When r is 1, the variables will move together perfectly in the same direction. In the example, we used annual data from 1990 to 2015 and the correlation between supply surplus and price for cotton is $r = -0.58$, which is a relatively strong negative correlation. Therefore, when supply exceeds demand by a greater amount, cotton prices decrease.

It is possible that high correlations between two variables occur just by chance, especially if the number of observations in the sample is low. In the cotton example, the sample size is 26 since the annual data covers the time period from 1990 through 2015. To determine if a regression will be useful for forecasting price is to test the statistical significance of the correlation. To do this test, we should compare the absolute value of r to the critical value of r, published in a statistical table or use a statistical calculator (www.socscistatistics.com). If the absolute value of r is greater than the critical value then the correlation is statistically significant at least $p < 0.05$, and a simple linear regression model can be developed. The lower the p-value the better. If the value of r is less than the critical value, then you should not proceed to do a simple linear regression.

So, what are the key steps in the correlation significance test? Significance tests assume data are normally distributed. This is likely to be the case if a large enough sample size is used. The most typical threshold of statistical significance is when the probability of the correlation is no greater than 5 percent (0.05). Because, based on logic, we know the expected direction of relationship between supply surplus and price (these should move in opposite directions), use a one-tailed test for significance.

The last piece of information needed to test for statistical significance is the degree of freedom. The degree of freedom is the number of observations in the sample minus two. In our example, it is the number of years observed (n) minus two. For cotton, we have data for 26 years, so the degree of freedom is $26 - 2 = 24$. Having more degrees of freedom reduces the critical value of r needed to be statistically significant. If possible, use 15 or more years of supply, demand, and price data. However, this may not be possible if there has been a recent major underlying change in the supply or demand for the commodity.

Using a Pearson correlation coefficient critical-value table for a one-tailed test, with a level of significance of 0.05, and 24 degrees of freedom, the critical value of r is 0.33. For cotton, the absolute value of r (0.57) is greater than the critical value. We conclude the relationship between supply surplus and price is statistically significant, and thus we can use simple linear regression to develop a statistical model to forecast price.

As discussed in Chapter 3, simple linear regression models are easily calculated using an Excel spreadsheet. Create a scatter chart between price and supply surplus. Price must be on the vertical (y) axis because it is the variable you want to predict based on supply surplus. In Excel using the layout tab, click on the data in the scatter chart, then insert a linear trend line and select the option to show the equation and the R^2 on the chart. The scatter graph and trend line for cotton are shown in Figure 4.5.

The R^2 indicates how well the regression line fits the data. If there is a poor fit, the regression line should not be used as a forecasting tool.

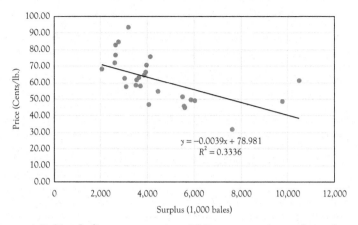

Figure 4.5 Simple linear regression: U.S. cotton price and surplus

Source: U.S. Department of Agriculture WASDE Report on Cotton.[31]

As explained in Chapter 3, an R^2 value of 1 indicates a perfect fit of the regression line to the data, and all the variance in the data is completely explained by the x-variable. Models with R^2 values close to 1 suggest the model will be helpful in forecasting price as long as nothing changes from the past. With real data, R^2 values are likely to be lower than 1. In Figure 4.5, for cotton, the R^2 of 0.33 shows only 33 percent of the variance in price is explained by the variance in surplus. Thus, although the model can be used to provide guidance it is limited in its predictive power.

To use the regression model to forecast price, which is the y value, enter your estimate of supply surplus as the x value. The assessment of the underlying factors affecting supply and demand provides the estimated value of supply surplus (x) to use in the equation. Assume you want to forecast the price of cotton in 2020 using the regression model shown in Figure 4.5. In 2015, the U.S. supply of cotton was 16,991 (1,000 bales). Based on the fundamental analysis cotton supply is expected to increase by 2 percent to 17,331 (1,000 bales) in 2020 relative to 2015. Demand in 2015 was 13,900 (1,000 bales), and it is estimated it will increase by 6 percent to 14,734 (1,000 bales) by 2015. Using these estimates, in 2015 the supply surplus is 17,330 − 14,734 = 2,597 (1,000 bales). This is the x value to use in the regression equation ($y = -0.0039x + 78.98$). Using the regression model, the forecast price of cotton is

(y = −0.0039(2,597) + 78.98), which comes to 68.85 cents/lb. Consider this price along with all other information you have and use your judgment to develop a final forecast for cotton in 2020.

Another variable often used to predict price, especially for agricultural commodities, is the stocks-to-use ratio. The stocks-to-use ratio is a percentage, calculated as the ending stock of a commodity in a time period (e.g., a year), divided by its total demand during the time period multiplied by 100. Figure 4.6 shows a scatter chart of cotton price on the y-axis and its stocks-to-use ratio on the x-axis. The correlation between price and the stocks-to-use ratio is r = −0.55. Comparing the absolute value of r (0.55) to the critical value of r (0.39), we conclude the correlation is statistically significant. Thus, a regression model can be developed and used to forecast price based on an estimate of stock to use for cotton.

Some words of caution for using simple linear regression modeling to develop long-term forecasts are in order. Linear regression uses historical data to predict the future. Thus, if there are changes in the fundamental underlying relationships between supply and demand, forecasts based on the regression model will be poor. Look again at Figure 4.1, which shows supply, demand, and price for natural gas. The development of shale gas technology fundamentally changed the supply market beginning in 2005. Thus combining data from before 2005 and after 2005 into a single model would be problematic. The fundamental shift was obvious in the

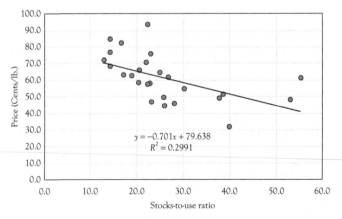

Figure 4.6 U.S. cotton price and stocks-to-use ratio, 1990 to 2015

Source: U.S. Department of Agriculture WASDE Report on Cotton.[32]

case for natural gas, but for other commodities the changes may be more difficult to identify.

Further, there may be outliers in the data. If you can clearly identify a reason for the outlier, for example perhaps the recession of 2008, you can exclude that data point from the analysis. If not, it would be best to include the data point in the analysis.

For some commodities, you may not find a correlation between price and supply surplus or price and the stocks-to-use ratio. There may be other factors influencing price that can be explored. For example, historically, oil and natural gas prices were correlated, but that is not necessarily the case today. More recently there is a high correlation between corn and oil prices because of the use of corn to make ethanol. If there is a factor highly correlated with price that you can estimate with reasonable accuracy, you can develop a regression equation and use it to help predict price.

Finally, supply and demand tell only part of the story for many commodities. For example, currency strength can affect prices for imported commodities. Price volatility also has been linked to trading activities. In recent years there are concerns that for some commodities, for example oil, prices are not that closely related to underlying supply and demand.[33] Thus, the fundamental forecasting process will be unique for each commodity.

Considering Future Prices

The commodity's futures prices should be examined before finalizing the long-term forecast. Futures contracts, as described in Chapters 5 and 9, are financial instruments in which buyers and sellers agree on the price for delivery of a commodity in the future. Buying a futures contract involves agreeing on a price to take delivery of a fixed amount of a commodity on the date specified by the contract. Sellers of futures contracts agree on a price to deliver a fixed amount of the commodity on the specified date.

Futures contracts are traded only in organized commodity exchanges such as the Chicago Mercantile Exchange (CME) or the London Metal Exchange (LME). There are many commodity exchanges all over the world. Since they are financial instruments, anyone can buy or sell futures contracts as long as they have money to cover a percent of the contract's value, called a margin. Futures contracts can be bought and sold many times before the delivery date. One confusing thing about futures contracts is the amount of the commodity traded in futures markets has no relationship with the actual amount of the commodity in the physical marketplace.

Futures contracts are standardized in terms of quantity, quality, trading months, and delivery dates. For example, the contract specifications for corn futures as traded on the CME is for 5,000 bushels of no. 2 yellow corn but includes price adjustments for other types of corn and has delivery in March, May, July, September, or December.[34] While there are futures available for a large number of agricultural products, metals, and energy products, not all commodities have futures contracts. However, commodities are added to the futures market frequently.

The participants in a futures market are either speculators or hedgers. Speculators are hoping to make money from making the correct decisions about price movements either up or down, and hedgers are hoping to reduce their exposure to price risk. Hedgers are producers or users of the actual commodity. In Chapters 5 and 9 we describe how supply chain managers can use hedging as one strategy to reduce exposure to price risk.

One of the key functions of the futures market is price discovery. Futures prices are not the same as the spot price that is paid for the actual physical commodity. The difference between the spot price and the futures price is called the spread or basis. Normally, the futures price is higher than the spot price because of uncertainty and inventory carrying costs. Occasionally, if the inventory of the physical commodity is unusually low, the futures price may be lower than the spot price.

Thus, futures prices can provide information about the expected trends for spot market prices for some commodities. Futures prices that are closer in time, within the next year to 18 months, tend to be traded at a higher volume and thus provide a better mirror into the price of the physical commodity. If the futures trading volume is low for a commodity, its futures price is not likely to reflect the market's perceptions about the actual physical commodity's price.

Further, futures prices are better predictors for some commodities than for others. Arbitrage, in which participants buy or sell in both the futures market and the physical market to profit from price differences, can distort futures prices for some commodities. Thus, determining how much weight to put on the futures prices in forecasting for a commodity requires reviewing the historical relationship between futures and spot prices. If these are closely related, the futures price may be a good predictor of the actual physical commodity's price.

Developing and Monitoring the Final Forecast

After completing the analysis, judgment is used to develop the forecast from a fundamental analysis. Judgment is needed to identify which supply and demand factors are important and how these factors will change supply and demand in the future. Statistical tools such as correlation and regression can be helpful but are not likely to provide a perfect, error-free forecast. For some commodities, futures prices suggest pricing trends but are not likely to reveal the commodity's exact price. To develop the final forecast you must weigh everything you have learned about the forecast, the qualitative data, predictions from linear regression models, and the futures price. All this information should be considered in deciding the final forecast. Unfortunately, there is no single magic formula that can be applied across commodities to develop a fundamental forecast. A deep understanding of a commodity's supply-and-demand markets and their relationships with price is necessary to be successful in long-term forecasting.

With a long-term forecast many things can happen between the time the forecast is developed and when the time period of interest arrives. Supply chain professionals need to continue to gather and monitor supply, demand, and price information after developing a forecast. When new information suggests it is needed, the forecast needs adjustment. Further, if the forecast has changed, managerial decisions based on the initial forecast need to be reviewed and possibly modified.

Summary

In this chapter, we describe an approach for using the market fundamentals of supply and demand to forecast a long-term price. To do a fundamental analysis, a wide range of information needs to be obtained to understand the basics about the commodity's supply and its demand. This is followed by identifying the key underlying factors affecting supply and demand. Determine which of those factors will affect supply and demand over the period forecasted and the type of change expected. With this information, an assessment of the percent change in supply and demand caused by these factors is determined for estimating the levels of supply and demand in the future.

The statistical tools of correlation and simple linear regression can be helpful in developing a forecast. Supply, demand, and price are plotted on the same line graph to find relationships. Supply surplus and stock-to-use ratios are two variables that may be related to price, but other variables such as stock levels or underlying factors may be more highly correlated with price. If a variable is found to be significantly correlated with price, then using simple linear regression to develop a model to forecast price is appropriate. If the commodity is traded in the futures market, consider the commodity's futures price and how it may predict the price of the physical commodity. Using judgment and all the information gathered about the commodity, a final forecast is made. The process is iterative in continuing to gather data and monitoring and adjusting the forecast, as well as any managerial decisions based on the forecast, as needed.

SECTION III

Managing Commodity Price Risk

CHAPTER 5

Managing Commodity Price Risk—Direct Commodity Purchases

Overview of Risk Characteristics and Approaches

This chapter builds on the overarching concepts discussed in Chapter 1, the assessment of risk exposure and risk tolerance influencing the effort needed for managing price risk discussed in Chapter 2, and the short- and long-term forecasts developed in Chapters 3 and 4 through technical and fundamental analysis, respectively. The approaches we propose in this chapter help you to select and implement an appropriate risk management strategy when you expect commodity prices for direct purchases to increase in the short-term, long-term, or both. We define a direct commodity purchase as one in which the commodity itself is transformed as part of the bill of materials in the products sold to customers. Commodities purchased by suppliers, which are transformed into components and subassemblies, construe value chain purchases. Approaches for managing the price volatility of value chain purchases are discussed in Chapter 6.

There are different approaches supply managers can use to manage price volatility with direct purchases, as shown in Figure 5.1. These are: (1) building in financial slack, (2) forward buying, (3) staggering contracts, (4) switching suppliers, (5) financial hedging, (6) cross-hedging, (7) improving product designs and production systems, and (8) developing a substitution strategy. Thus, there is a certain degree of flexibility in selecting the best approach for each specific situation.

Some of the approaches are most appropriate for the short-term, while others are better applied in the long run. Short-term alternatives include purchasing a larger amount to cover known future needs—using forward buying, substituting approved materials in the bill of materials,

Approach	Description
Developing a substitution strategy	Substituting commodities concerns the ability of the purchasing firm and/or suppliers to use different materials in the product, based up on the price movements of the commodity itself.
Improving product designs and production systems	Redesigning products, processes, and packaging can sometimes significantly reduce the demand for a commodity, lowering spend and reducing exposure to price risk. Continuous improvement is often used by some companies to reduce the quantity of the commodity used in the product or the amount of scrap generated in the production process.
Cross-hedging	Cross-hedging is used to offset price risk with a commodity that has similar price movements in situations in which no commodity exchange exists or the market liquidity for a commodity's financial derivatives is low.
Financial hedging	Financial hedging consists of acquiring futures, options or other derivatives to offset anticipated future commodity price increases. This strategy is typically used for commodities with a rich history of trading in financial markets, and with high futures market liquidity.
Switching suppliers	Supplier switching means moving purchases among approved suppliers for the commodity. With this strategy companies tend to have long-term agreements in place with suppliers but flexibility within the contract to shift volumes among these suppliers.
Staggering contracts	Staggering contracts are used for different quantities and times. To reduce risk, firms can use fixed-price contracts that are staggered throughout the year, with more contracts locked in as the time for the actual material purchase approaches.
Forward buying	Forward buying is almost always focused on short-term needs, and more often implemented as a method to assure supply continuity rather than in response to anticipated price increases.
Building in financial slack	Building-in financial slack consists of ensuring an internal retention—through the allocation of founds in the balance sheet or in the purchasing budget—for covering extra costs related to unexpected negative fluctuations of commodity prices.

High   Complexity   Low

Figure 5.1 Approaches for managing commodity price volatility—direct purchases

and using alternative energy sources in operations. Long-term decisions, regarding commodity price risk management, can include hedging using futures contracts to offset price movements, negotiating contractual escalator clauses with suppliers and customers to share the risk burden, and modifying product designs and production processes to provide sourcing flexibility. Further, several of the long-term approaches facilitate the execution of short-term ones. For example, substituting materials in the bill of materials or energy sources is a short-term approach for managing commodity price risk. However, this approach is not possible without first developing flexible product designs and production processes, which often takes time and a significant amount of resources.

In the remainder of this chapter, the viability and effectiveness of each technique are discussed in depth from the buying-firm's perspective. The approaches are discussed in order from the least to the most complex to implement. Several factors affect complexity, including the skills needed and the number of different business functions and firms that should be involved in decision making. For example, some approaches can be implemented quickly by one supply chain professional while others require cross-functional participation and approval, and some need cross-organizational inputs, from suppliers, customers, third parties, nongovernmental organizations (NGOs), governments, consumers, and other key stakeholders. Resource requirements, a third factor contributing to complexity, can include the amount of personnel time consumed in analysis and decision making, monitoring, the use of third parties, various approval processes, accounting documents, capital equipment, setup times, additional inventory, transaction costs, and negotiating and relationship costs.

Building in Financial Slack

Building-in financial slack consists of creating additional financial "slack" to absorb the risks related to unexpected cost increases, including commodity price increases. This is possible by ensuring an internal retention—through the allocation of funds in the balance sheet or in the purchasing budget—of extra costs related to unexpected negative fluctuations of commodity prices. When there are exceptional variations in raw material prices or component prices, these fluctuations are absorbed by contingencies or transferred into the final price of the product. These decisions are often the provenance of the finance department, working with supply management. In the case of price increases, sales and marketing must agree to the decision. A firm implementing this approach must also have the luxury of being in an industry or niche where attaining high-margins allow firms to have more slack than companies in low-margin industries, such as many food product and packaging firms.

Forward Buying

Forward buying involves acquiring commodities well in advance of anticipated need during times when prices are considered very favorable but are forecast to increase in the future. A forward buy locks in the prices of future purchases. Companies such as Caterpillar buy materials in advance.[1] In another example, an office-furniture manufacturer reduced the prices paid for steel in the short-term from a forward buy.[2] This company purchased as much steel as it could buy in response to forecasted price increases during the fourth quarter of 2004. As a result, its inventories of steel increased 15 percent before it was put on allocation by suppliers. This allowed the firm to ensure steel availability for the production of office furniture as business was ramping up, while also paying a lower price for steel.

Forward buys are possible if firms acquire commodities via spot market purchases and have the capital and capability to acquire and store the material. However, there are several distinct disadvantages to this strategy. Forward buys are not compatible with lean supply chain practices. Inventory held because of forward buys ties up capital, hides potential operating problems, increases storage and handling costs, and increases the chance for damage, obsolesce, and spoilage. In addition, forward buys are based on forecasts, and if the prices decrease rather than increase, your firm may have higher costs than competitors who use a different risk management strategy. In addition, it is largely impractical for perishable commodities. For these reasons, firms need to carefully analyze the price advantage relative to cost before forward buying, given uncertain future prices.

Forward buying is almost always focused on short-term needs, and more often implemented as a method to assure supply continuity rather than in response to anticipated price increases. Firms engaging in forward buying often use it selectively, and for very specific commodities. For example, a food manufacturer we have worked with uses forward buying only when financial hedging or contract agreements cannot be used.

To determine if a forward buy is a viable option, ask if your organization has the capability or desire to hold additional inventory for a period of time. This often depends on how the commodity is consumed in the organization, whether it is part of the bill of materials, or if it is used in support of other activities or processes. For example, Hershey Foods investigated the feasibility of buying, storing, and subsequently distributing diesel fuel through a volume-leveraged purchase agreement as one strategy for managing fuel surcharges passed on by its carriers.[3] Although Hershey Foods had some ability to store fuel, it did not have the capacity to meet the full requirements of its carriers. This strategy raised other issues outside the scope of the company's capabilities, such as managing fuel distribution and getting the fuel to the appropriate carriers and trucks, all while conducting these operations effectively and efficiently.

If your firm has the capability, both in terms of finances as well as in physical resources to purchase larger stock quantities in advance of actual need, a cost–benefit analysis is absolutely essential. If the results of cost–benefit analysis are not favorable, other risk management approaches may be more appropriate.

Staggering Contracts

Staggering contracts by using contracts for different quantities and time periods is another way to manage commodity price volatility. To reduce risk, one of the firms we studied uses fixed-price contracts staggered throughout the year, with more contracts locked in as the time for the actual material purchase approaches. Generally, about one quarter prior to the start of production, 100 percent of its contracts are locked in at fixed prices.

Among different contractual agreements, companies often use escalator clauses, which will be described in Chapter 6. By using these clauses, companies can adjust commodity prices with their suppliers or customers. The extent of the adjustment is defined during the contract negotiation, as long as the time periods and quantities.

Switching Suppliers

Switching suppliers is also sometimes done to reduce commodity prices. This technique is simply moving purchases among approved suppliers for the commodity. The companies engaging in supplier switching tend to have long-term agreements in place with suppliers but flexibility within the contract to shift volumes among these suppliers. Although this approach may be viewed as transactional, we have noticed in our research some of the companies implementing this approach emphasize the importance of maintaining long-term relationships with a limited number of prequalified suppliers that can meet their quality, delivery, and other requirements. Therefore, even though there is switching among suppliers, due to temporary price changes, buying firms using this approach have some flexibility by being able to "shop" for the lower price, given all else is equal.

Financial Hedging

Financial hedging consists of acquiring futures, options or other derivatives to offset anticipated future commodity price increases. Firms engaging in this practice utilize financial instruments solely as a risk management approach, and not as a speculative tool. Firms utilizing this approach frequently create highly structured decision-making processes, often requiring executive approval for use. This approach is mainly used for high-volume purchases, and hence, as described in Chapter 2, is only merited when there is significant spend, high risk exposure, and high price volatility. However, in our research, we have also found although these three conditions hold, some firms prefer not to participate in financial hedging because of the nature of their purchases or due to the lack of knowledge and experience with this strategy.

One of the primary drivers for financial hedging appears to be associated with established industry practices. For example, we have discovered many firms in the food production industry using financial hedging to a significant extent to offset price increases for agricultural products such as coffee, wheat, and corn. These commodities have a rich history of trading in financial markets and are clearly defined with regard to their specifications, and generally have high futures market liquidity.

A futures contract is a financial tool, which is an agreement between two parties to buy or sell a commodity at a particular time in the future for a particular price. Contracts are standardized with respect to quality, quantity, delivery time, and delivery location. The only variable is price, which is determined by trading in organized commodity exchanges. One of the most popular exchanges in the United States is the Chicago Mercantile Exchange (CME; www.cmegroup.com), which trades contracts for a variety of agriculture, energy, and metal commodities. The intention of a futures contract is to be a financial instrument, not a primary source of the physical commodity, and very few of the futures contracts created actually result in delivery.

There are two types of participants in the futures markets: speculators and hedgers. Speculators do not produce or use the actual commodity but instead are trying to profit by correctly forecasting a commodity's price movements and then buying or selling futures contracts at the right time. Depending on their beliefs about the direction of price movements, speculators will either buy or sell futures contracts now and do the opposite transaction later, before the contract's delivery date, in hopes of making a profit. Assume, as a speculator in July 2016, prices for March 2017 corn futures are $4.35/bushel, but you expect prices to increase to a higher level before March. You buy corn futures now with the intention of selling them at a higher price before the delivery date of March 2017. If in January 2017, futures prices increase to $4.45/bushel, you sell the futures for a difference of $0.10/bushel. By selling the contract before its due date, your obligation to take delivery of the physical commodity is canceled.

Hedgers, who are producers or users of a commodity, participate in the futures market to reduce exposure to price risk. Hedging is possible because for commodities, prices in the futures market and the spot market tend to move parallel to each other. Normally though, futures prices are higher than the price in the spot market until it gets close to the delivery month. So how does hedging work? Take for example, farmers who face the risk of a price decrease from the time they plant their crops until the crops are harvested and sold. To reduce this risk, farmers hedge by selling futures contracts now and buying the contracts back at a lower price near harvest time. The gain in the futures market offsets the loss from the price decrease in the physical market. Users of a commodity face the risk of a price increase from the time they contract with their customers until the commodity is actually purchased. To hedge, users of a commodity buy futures contracts now and then sell them later, before the due date, when the price has increased. Again, the gain in the futures market offsets the loss from the increased price when the physical commodity is purchased.

To clarify the hedging process, let's review a simple example summarized in Table 5.1. A snack food company purchases large amounts of corn to produce tortilla chips. In October, the company enters into a contract with a large grocery chain to delivery tortilla chips for a Cinco de Mayo promotion the following May. The snack food company's supply chain manager needs to purchase 52,000 bushels of corn in March to meet the May delivery date. Forecasts suggest the price of corn will rise from its current spot price of $4.25/bushel in October, which was used as the basis of pricing the tortilla chips to the grocery chain. The snack food company does not have the space to forward buy and store corn in inventory. Instead, in October, the company buys 10 corn futures contracts (5,000 bushel per contract) for a May 2017 delivery at a price of $4.35/bushel. As expected, the price of corn increases in both the futures and spot markets. In March, the price for May 2017 corn futures is $4.55/bushel. The company sells the futures contracts and buys corn in the spot market at the prevailing price of $4.50/bushel. The gain in the futures transaction is $0.20/bushel ($4.55/bushel—$4.35/bushel). The loss in the spot market

Table 5.1 Hedging example

	Physical (spot) market	Futures market
October 2016	Price product to customer based on corn spot price of $4.25/bushel	Buy 10 May 2017 corn futures (50,000 bushel per contract) at $4.35/bushel
March 2017	Buy 52,000 bushels of corn at $4.50/bushel	Sell 10 corn futures at $4.55/bushel
Gain/loss	Loss of $0.25/bushel	Gain of $0.20/bushel

is $0.25/bushel, which is the price paid ($4.50/bushel) minus the price in October ($4.25/bushel) that was the basis of the pricing to the customer. The hedging-transaction gain reduced the overall loss from $0.25/bushel to $0.05/bushel. The actual loss to the organization will be slightly more than $0.05/bushel because the gain from hedging must be reduced by its transaction costs. These costs include broker's fees and the cost of capital for the money needed to purchase the futures contracts.

After reviewing this example, the natural question is, why didn't the snack food company buy corn futures for March 2017 and take delivery of the corn? There are several reasons this may not be practical. The most important one is the company has no control over the type or quality of corn received. The CME contract specifications for corn futures state the corn delivered could be one of three different grades of corn.[4] For many products, the grade and even variation within a grade are important factors influencing an end product's quality. The snack food company most likely has developed partnerships with key corn growers to ensure the corn they receive consistently meets its product specifications. Thus, rather than taking delivery from a random source, the snack food company would rather buy from its partner growers.

The delivery time frame, amount, and location are also problematic for futures contracts. The delivery date for corn futures traded on the CME is the second business day following the last trading day of the month, and there are five trading months: September, December, March, May, and July.[5] Many futures contracts are not traded every month. So the date when the commodity is available for delivery may not be when it is needed. The amount of commodity delivered is fixed by the contract specifications. For example, corn futures contracts are traded and require delivery in increments of 5,000 bushels. In our example, the snack food company needed 52,000 bushels, so it would be 2,000 bushels short if it took delivery on the futures contracts. Another problem is the delivery locations are specified by the commodity exchange. The buyer must arrange and pay for transporting the commodity from the delivery location to their facility. The cost of transportation can be much higher than if the commodity was sourced locally. Thus, for most commodities, the futures markets are used simply as financial instruments, and the actual physical commodity is purchased in the spot market.

One benefit of hedging compared to forward buying is cash flow. For example, to forward buy a commodity, a company must pay for the entire amount of the commodity when it is purchased. To buy or sell futures contracts, only a percent of the actual purchase price is tied up. Opening an account with a commodities broker requires a deposit of a percent of the overall cost of the futures contract. This deposit is called an initial margin or performance bond. The initial margin is established by the commodity exchange following government regulations. Commodities with higher levels of price risk typically have higher margins. A futures contract for soybeans traded on the CME is for 5,000 bushels, and the price for May 2017 delivery is $10.89/bushel (on June 15, 2016). The actual total cost of this contract is $54,430, but to open the account to buy or sell futures, you only need to put up the initial margin of $4,477 per contract ($2,300 maintenance plus 0.04 maintenance volume times contract cost) as required by the CME.[6] As you own the contract, the daily settlement prices change, and the account will be debited or credited based on the price movements. However, if the amount in the account drops below the maintenance margin level, which for soybeans is $2,300, then money must be deposited to bring the account back up to the initial margin level.[7]

In this subsection, we have described financial hedging using futures contracts. Futures options can also be used for hedging. An option is the right to buy or sell a specific amount of futures at a specific price and during a specific time frame. As hedging with futures or options is a complex process, it is important to work with the finance department in designing and implementing a hedging strategy in order to attain the greatest outcomes for managing price volatility. Additional information associated with hedging strategies is discussed in Chapter 9—Further Insights on Financial Hedging Instruments.

Cross-Hedging

Cross-hedging is used to offset price risk with a commodity having similar price movements in situations in which no commodity exchange exists or the market liquidity for a commodity's financial derivatives is low. However, the use of cross-hedging has specific legal requirements that must be met in order to implement it as a risk management tool, thereby limiting the extent to which it is deployed. In our research we have observed only a few organizations experienced in cross-hedging.

One of the limitations with hedging using futures contracts is some commodities are not traded in futures markets. Thus, it is not possible to directly hedge these commodities. In these situations, you need to identify a commodity traded in futures whose price movements are strongly related to the movements of the actual physical commodity the company purchases. For example, prior to 2007, diesel fuel was not traded on the futures market.[8] When the price of diesel began to increase in 2001, Hershey's looked for a substitute commodity it could use for hedging. Managers found the price movements of diesel fuel were highly correlated with those of heating oil, which was traded on the New York Mercantile Exchange (NYMEX), and thus heat oil was a good candidate for cross-hedging.[9]

The first step with cross-hedging is to identify commodities whose price movements may be similar to the commodity of interest. Use correlation and regression (described in Chapter 4) to understand the strength of the relationship between historical prices of the two commodities, ideally over at least a 10-year period. If a high correlation is found, then do a fundamental analysis of both commodities (also described in Chapter 4) to estimate the probability the historical relationship is likely to continue in the future. If so, use the commodity for cross-hedging.

Another consideration is how many futures contracts to buy for hedging. Even if you find the prices of two commodities are highly correlated, it is highly unlikely the two commodities will be exactly the same price. Hershey's found diesel fuel was about twice as expensive as heating oil.[10] Thus, the company purchased heating oil futures in the value covering the total spend in diesel fuel.

Improving Product/Production Designs and Systems

In the long-term, organizations can reduce their exposure to price risk by reducing or eliminating their need for the commodity by improving product designs and production and supply chain systems. For example, many organizations have installed new lighting fixtures that use energy-efficient light bulbs and sensors that turn off lights when they are not in use to reduce electricity consumption. Redesign of products, processes, and packaging can significantly reduce the demand for a commodity, lowering spend and reducing exposure to price risk. In 2007, Arrowhead redesigned its water bottle, so they use 30 percent less plastic yet are functional and have a high level of consumer acceptance.[11] Reducing demand for commodities also is consistent with environmental sustainability initiatives.

Continuous improvement is used by some companies to reduce the quantity of the commodity used in the product or the amount of scrap generated in the production process. Commodity price increases for direct purchases, as well as the content in supplier components, can motivate companies to reduce their consumption. For example, several companies we have studied redesigned products to use a lower grade of steel or reduce the thickness of a part to reduce the amount of aluminum used. Continuous improvement appears to be a less frequently utilized tool for commodity price risk management. However, this may also be a by-product of companies' pursuits of lean initiatives.

Product and process innovation requires collaboration, both internally with various functions, and externally, with supply chain partners. The redesign of products and processes to reduce commodity demand may require a large investment in research and development, marketing research, and capital equipment. However, if successful, reducing demand for the commodity will subsequently reduce the organization's exposure to price risk.

Developing a Substitution Strategy

Substituting commodities concerns the ability of the purchasing firm and suppliers to use different materials in the product based on the price movements of the commodity itself. The strategy for commodity substitution is appropriate for both direct commodity and value chain purchases, with its application for direct commodity purchases discussed here. Ideally, the different commodities should be preapproved so they can be easily switched. For example, some coffee producers routinely switch between Arabica and Robusta coffee beans based on price. However, easily switching from one commodity to another is often not technically feasible or economically viable. When sourcing tires for its products, one of the firms we have studied allows its tire suppliers to change the percentage mix of styrene butadiene rubber and natural rubber quantities within strict bounds, based in part on the prices of these commodities. The actual tire formulation is left to the suppliers' discretion as long as they stay within the agreed-upon specifications. Examples in the food production industry include flexibility in the ratios of butter and milk powder used, and switching between sugar and other types of sweeteners.

In most cases, we found switching from one commodity to another requires engineering design and extensive testing to confirm the product with the new material meets performance requirements. It is absolutely essential that prior approval is obtained from customers, including the final consumer, in these types of decisions—and no detrimental technical effects result from the substitution. In addition, new equipment and tooling are often needed. For example, a firm we worked with encourages its customers to switch their products to a resin having a more stable price. However, this switch is not a painless one; for one thing, there are some technical advantages to the current resin relative to the alternative resins. If the resin is switched on an existing product, new molds are needed. Further, prior to switching, customers have to conduct tests to confirm the products perform to their specifications. Because of these challenges, customers are reluctant to move forward.

Thus, switching commodities is a longer term approach that is evaluated and considered during product development. For example, the substitution of materials (e.g., aluminum, light-weight materials, rare earth elements) takes place based on long-term forecasts for some firms in the automotive industry where their supply management teams can still influence the final product/bill of material. Such substitution is a key commodity price risk management activity during the development phase of a car line. Another firm we have studied redesigns its parts to replace metal with plastic, but with the primary purpose is to meet customer-mandated weight reduction goals. However, switching to different materials can also reduce price volatility.

In some cases, substitute materials have not been approved by the organization. In this situation, you must provide strong supporting evidence of the viability of substitution, by comparing the historical price patterns of potential substitutes to those of the approved commodity. For substitution to be effective, the historical prices of the approved and substitute commodities must intersect and preferably be strongly negatively correlated, so when one commodity's price is lower, the other is higher. However, a negative correlation is not necessary, since prices of two commodities can still intersect.

The ability and expertise to substitute materials in product or production process design almost always requires the internal input, buy-in, support, cooperation, and integration from multiple business functions, as well as supply chain partners. Typically, product design, marketing, operations, purchasing, and logistics are involved in developing and implementing a successful substitution strategy for managing commodity price risk.

Design engineers—both internally, within the firm, and externally, if designs are solicited and purchased from other firms—serve a critical role for developing the capability to change material inputs in a product's design. Marketing and sales are also key business functions to include in determining the viability of employing a substitution strategy for managing commodity price risk. The marketing function should understand and incorporate the "voice of the customer" in determining the appropriateness of various materials in the bill of materials.

For manufacturing, questions include these: How does the substitute material affect production through input and capacity utilization? Does the current production equipment allow for the use of substitute materials? What are the effects on production process quality and yield? Is there an increase or decrease in labor time or other costs, such as processing costs?

The supply management function often has the primary oversight for understanding suppliers and the industries those suppliers compete, and it should definitely have a "seat at the table" when considering substitute materials. For example, design engineers may be able to identify a substitute material that can be incorporated as an option in the bill of materials for a product. However, they may or may not have the requisite knowledge of the market dynamics of potential material substitutes. Are there potential threats of supply disruptions? Are the materials available only from a limited number of suppliers or regions of the world? How do the prices move in relation to other candidate materials? Are these materials already purchased for different applications, and if so, what are the potential effects of volume increases (or decreases) on the overall total costs of purchases from suppliers?

In conjunction with supply management, logistics should also be solicited for input on substitution decisions. Are there any import restrictions or tariffs with regard to the candidate substitute material? Do current or potential carriers have the capability of switching routes in a cost-effective manner? Should alternative transportation modes be considered, and how does this influence the flow of material and inventory levels?

An analysis of external forces and supply chain dynamics and relationships is just as important as the internal influences of other business functions in determining the appropriateness and viability of executing a substitution strategy. These include considering the effects of suppliers at multiple tiers in the upstream (supplier-facing) supply chain, customer acceptance, competitor reactions, governmental policies, and even the effect on the natural environment.

Summary

This chapter provides a discussion of approaches and techniques you can implement for managing price risk associated with direct commodity purchases. There is "no one size fits all" approach for managing price fluctuations of direct commodity purchases. Firm size, supply management expertise, customer requirements, and a myriad of other factors influence the ability and availability of approaches for mitigating this risk. The approaches described in this chapter are provided in order of complexity or difficulty in implementation. The more complex processes are generally, the more expensive they are to conduct. Hence, why, it is imperative to determine, as outlined in Chapter 2, whether it is cost-effective for managing commodity price volatility, and which approaches provide the best value for firms to implement, given an uncertain future price.

Firms are exposed to commodity price volatility and its risk not just from their direct commodity purchases, but are also frequently vulnerable to risk associated with supplier exposure to price fluctuations in their direct purchases of commodities (second-tier supply sources from the firm's perspective). Approaches and tools for managing this form of price risk are discussed in the next chapter.

CHAPTER 6

Managing Commodity Price Risk—Value Chain Purchases

Overview of Risk Characteristics and Approaches

In Chapter 5, we examined various approaches firms can implement for managing commodity price risk from direct commodity purchases. However, risk exposure can come from other sources, such as energy purchases, packaging, transportation, as well as from upstream in supply chains from commodities purchased by suppliers. For example, in the trucking industry, passing on price increases to customers in the form of fuel surcharges is a common practice.[1]

The focus of this chapter is to examine several approaches you can consider for managing commodity price volatility stemming from the commodity purchases made by your component and subassembly suppliers in your value/supply chains. These approaches include creating firm fixed-price contracts, piggyback contracting, inserting escalation/de-escalation clauses in contracts, improving product designs and production processes with suppliers, and vertically integrating as shown in Figure 6.1.

Similar to Chapter 5, we have ordered the various approaches for managing commodity price volatility by their level of complexity in implementation and execution, from easiest to most difficult. There are several factors as well, related with and beyond complexity, influencing which approach to use. One factor, supply chain expertise, partly influences the choice of approach for managing commodity price volatility with supplier purchases. Approaches such as utilizing firm fixed-price contracts and piggy back contracting are rarely complex, and can often be accomplished solely by the supply management function of the firm without too much difficulty. However, improving products and processes

Approach	Description
Vertically integrating	*Vertical integration* is an approach in which an organization owns its distribution channels or production of its raw materials. In this approach firms can decide to produce raw materials in-house, or may choose to buy from vertically integrated suppliers to avoid price volatility from market exposure. This is a strategic decision that requires a commitment of capital, increases the assets of the firm, and increases managerial complexity.
Improving supplier products/processes	Organizations can improve their respective products and production processes to reduce commodity demand, and hence commodity price risk. This strategy can be implemented for value chain purchases, for example by encouraging and rewarding suppliers to continually improve product design and production processes to reduce, in part, the content of a commodity used.
Inserting escalation/de-escalation clauses	The use of escalation clauses is decided when developing contract clauses. In particular, the organization defines how often the prices are reviewed and changed, the base "cost/price" from which adjustments will be made, what the prices will be compared to, if past or future prices will be changed, and if there are upper and lower limits (bands) between which no price adjustments will be made.
Piggy-back contracting	Piggy-back contracting is an approach in which an organization enters into contracts with upstream commodity suppliers for a specific purchase volume and price. With directed sourcing, the organization's first-tier suppliers are then required to purchase their commodities off of this contract.
Creating firm fixed price contracts	Firm fixed-price contracts are used to ensure supply, reduce administrative costs, and are sometimes required by customers. However, some suppliers are not willing to enter into fixed-price contracts because they bear all the price risk. Further, suppliers with limited resources, lower margins, and lack of risk management expertise may not be able to absorb or effectively manage price risk.

High ← Complexity → Low

Figure 6.1 Approaches for managing commodity price volatility—direct purchases

or vertically integrating operations are almost always complex. These are cross-functional and cross-organizational strategic processes many firms may not necessarily have the all of expertise, influence, or resources to execute.

A second factor influencing the adoption of risk mitigation approaches is the power in the supply chain. For example, in the competitive appliance industry Whirlpool finds it very difficult to fully pass on material price increases to customers without losing market share to foreign rivals.[2] In the automobile industry, it has been estimated that steel represents approximately 4 percent of the cost of a car, for example, $1,000 of a $25,000 car. A 20 to 30 percent rise in steel costs would have a parallel cost increase of $200, but many companies in this industry would be more likely to absorb those increases than to pass on those costs to consumers and thereby potentially lose business. In our cases, we found that in the chemical industry organizations chose to pass commodity price increases to customers only for innovative products, and are likely to absorb raw material prices for standardized products.

Several approaches require the buyer to exert some degree of influence on the supplier or customer. Approaches such as inserting escalation/de-escalation clauses and improving products and processes often require significant supplier (or customer) input and "buy-in," which may not happen if the buyer has limited influence within the supply chain. The buying firm's size and amount of spend also influence the selection of commodity risk management approaches for value chain purchases. Small organizations, and those with limited spend levels may not have the resources available to engage in approaches such as directed sourcing contracts or vertically integrating to manage commodity price volatility.

Creating Firm Fixed-Price Contracts

Firm fixed-price contracts are used to ensure supply, reduce administrative costs, and are sometimes required by customers. Two firms that we have studied use firm fixed-price contracts with some suppliers to ensure supply. Food manufacturers can face supply challenges because farmers often switch among crops to improve their margins; by guaranteeing a specific price, companies can ensure that suppliers will grow the specific crops that they need. Another firm that we have worked with uses firm fixed-price contracts with its low-spend suppliers to reduce the administrative costs associated with price changes. However, some suppliers are not willing to enter into fixed-price contracts because they bear all the price risk. Further, suppliers with limited resources, lower margins, and lack of risk management expertise may not be able to absorb or effectively manage price risk. When prices increase, these suppliers may lower costs in other areas reducing quality or delivery performance, exit the business, or even potentially become bankrupt—all of which negatively impact the buyer. This is especially true in circumstances where buyers have limited options in finding and selecting new supply sources.

Piggyback Contracting

Piggyback contracting is an approach in which an organization enters into contracts with upstream commodity suppliers for a specific purchase volume and price. With piggyback contracts, the organization's first-tier suppliers are then required to purchase their commodities off of this contract. If the organization spends a significant amount on the commodity and is able to take advantage of volume leverage purchases, then the supplier, who also requires that commodity, may be able to "piggyback" off your contract. In this case, the purchasing organization acquires enough of the commodity to meet its requirements, as well as those of the supplier, and thereby assumes the price risk of the commodity. This approach is often used when the buyer uses a much higher level of the commodity than its suppliers. If your organization has more resources and expertise in understanding the commodity and managing price risk than your suppliers, this may be an attractive alternative.

There are several benefits to this approach. Volumes can be combined across suppliers so volume discounts can be obtained. In addition, the buyer knows the actual price that is being paid for the commodity and thus has a better understanding of the supplier's cost structure. In our research we have found several firms implementing this approach, particularly for mitigating price fluctuations of commodities such as steel, aluminum, and several oil-derived products. These companies use piggyback contracting almost always with component suppliers that are much smaller in size and influence as compared to the buyer. This approach is often used in conjunction with other approaches, such as escalation/ de-escalation clauses and financial hedging, since the approach does not necessarily mitigate the price risk, but often instead provides the purchasing firm greater price transparency and control for managing commodity price volatility exposure from supplier firms.

Including Escalation Clauses and Formula Pricing in Contracts

Negotiating escalation/de-escalation clauses in contractual agreements with suppliers and customers is a common approach for managing commodity price volatility. The escalation clause might relate to commodity price variations or labor costs but our discussion focuses on commodity prices. Key decisions that must be made when developing contract clauses include how often the prices are reviewed and changed, the base cost/price from which adjustments will be made, what the prices will be compared to, if past or future prices will be changed, and if there are upper and lower limits (bands) between which no price adjustments will be made. These decisions must be agreed upon when negotiating contracts with customers or suppliers.

Escalator/de-escalator clauses with suppliers are generally reviewed and adjusted monthly or quarterly. The decision on the frequency of review and price adjustment requires analyzing the trade-off between administrative costs and responsiveness to price changes. For example, price changes are typically made manually in enterprise resource planning (ERP) or e-procurement systems. Reducing the frequency of these changes—quarterly rather than monthly, for example—may have a positive impact on administrative costs for the buyer and suppliers. A drawback with less frequent changes is that the time lag between the actual prices paid and the adjustment, which can be a concern when prices are highly volatile.

Our research suggests that prices are reviewed and adjusted with customers once or twice a year. The frequency of price changes with customers is based on factors such as overall cost structures, market conditions, and competitor behaviors. When reviews are less frequent, buyers depend more on forecasted commodity prices to determine their overall pricing strategy. Inaccuracies in forecasted commodity prices can detrimentally affect overall profitability of products and product lines, since prices charged to customers are fixed for a period of time.

Another factor that must be agreed upon is the base price of the component that will be adjusted. It is important to determine the amount of the commodity in the part or component and the initial purchase price. The point of reference for the price adjustment also needs to be negotiated. Typically published indices such as those on the London Metals Exchange or other commodity markets are used. The index may change depending upon the location of the supplier. To reduce administrative costs, price bands can also be negotiated. For example, a price band of 5 percent means that the price must increase or decrease more than 5 percent relative to the initial price before any adjustment is made.

Let's review an example of how the price adjustment process works. Assume a company manufactures wiring harnesses and just signed a 2-year contract to provide those components starting February 1, 2016, for a specialty heavy equipment transportation manufacturer. The negotiated price for the wiring harnesses is $100 each, and each component contains five pounds of copper. Copper is purchased by the wiring harness manufacturer in the spot market once a month, and due to manufacturing lead times, 1 month prior to delivery of the component. Contract terms for payment are net 30, and deliveries are scheduled on the first of every month, or the next workday if the first of the month is on a holiday or a weekend.

An escalator clause was negotiated to share the burden or benefits of copper price increases or decreases, respectively, if they rise or decrease by more than 5 percent from the initial Copper Futures cash spot price observed on January 1, which was $2.06 (U.S. dollars). Further, during negotiation, it was agreed that the purchase price would be re-evaluated on a monthly basis on the first of the month or the next appropriate workday. The buyer and supplier agreed to share any change in price 50/50.

Table 6.1 shows how purchase prices are adjusted based on the escalator clause. The purchase price for the February 1st delivery date is $100 per wiring harness, since the copper price is based on the original negotiated purchase price of $2.06. However, as can be seen for February 1, the copper cash price increased to $2.13, a 3.40 percent difference from the January copper spot price. Since this 3.40 percent difference does not exceed the 5 percent threshold, no price adjustment is made.

Table 6.1 *Purchase price changes based on copper cash prices (US$)*

Date (2016)	Price (US$)	Percent difference from January (%)	Price change to share after 5 percent threshold	Burden share per pound	Total price increase	Modified price
January 1	$2.06					
February 1	$2.13	3.40	NA	NA	NA	100
March 1	$2.18	5.83	0.02	0.01	0.05	100.05
April 1	$2.28	10.68	0.12	0.06	0.3	100.30
May 1	$2.10	1.94	NA	NA	NA	NA

Source: www.investing.com/commodities/copper-historical-data[3]

In continuing this example to the next month, we can see that the price of copper on March 1 rose again to $2.18 in preparation to meet the customer order on April 1. Compared with the price on January 1, this is an increase of $0.12 per pound, or a 5.8 percent difference, thereby exceeding the requirement of a 5 percent increase or decrease. For five pounds of copper per wiring harness this comes to a total cost increase of copper of $0.05. Since it was agreed to split copper price increases or decreases evenly, or 50/50, the overall total price increase would be $0.05 or a sales/purchase price of $100.05 (rounding up in this example) for a March 1st delivery and payment on April 1.

As we can see from this example, it is imperative to select an appropriate index or price source. Whichever one is selected should be the one that best reflects the actual spot price increases the supplier pays and can even include their actual purchase prices, if you are confident in the sourcing process and expertise of the supplier.

Revisiting Improving Product/Production Designs and Systems

In Chapter 5, we discussed how organizations can improve their respective products and production processes to reduce commodity demand, thereby reducing the firms' overall financial exposure to price fluctuations. Improving product designs and production processes, however, is not limited or constrained to just direct commodity purchases, but can also be implemented for value chain purchases. Although this approach can be implemented regardless of exposure to increasing commodity prices, it is the threat and concern of commodity price volatility that can serve as an impetus for pursuing continuous improvement initiatives.

Several companies that we have studied have many of their supply chain professionals participating on various commodity teams. Within these teams, conference calls are made every one to two weeks to look at raw materials, which often extends beyond operations and often includes suppliers. For example, one firm has reduced its inventory levels of steel from several weeks to approximately two days of supply on hand. However, with regard to other commodity price risk management strategies, this process improvement has eliminated their ability to forward buy due to a lack of inventory space.

Another approach used in the value chain is to encourage and reward suppliers to continually improve product design and production processes to reduce, in part, the content of a commodity used. For example, another firm we studied works with radiator suppliers in finding ways to use less material, which also often results in reduced equipment weight. In another example, a firm we have worked with continually considers product and process redesigns to increase vehicle fuel efficiency, with a side benefit of reducing commodity price risk. Many of this firm's products were designed decades ago using zinc, aluminum and steel. Most of the zinc parts have been converted to aluminum to reduce weight and improve vehicle fuel efficiency.

In addition, this company has been successfully redesigning metal parts to be made out of plastic. One challenge is that plastic prices are also volatile, and there is no standard index to use with it as there is with steel and aluminum. The approach being used with plastics part suppliers is that the supplier notifies this firm of a planned price change 90 days in advance and the two companies then negotiate the price change. In addition, they work with suppliers to use different grades of materials that are lower cost. Similarly, they evaluate whether the thickness of a part or its overall design can be changed to reduce weight and improve part manufacturing. The primary reason for this is to reduce weight, but it also reduces the amount of raw materials in the part, and hence, financial exposure to commodity price volatility.

Vertically Integrating

Vertical integration is an approach in which an organization owns its distribution channels or production of raw materials. In this approach firms can decide to produce raw materials in-house, or may choose to buy from vertically integrated suppliers to avoid price volatility from market exposure.[4] This is a strategic decision that requires a commitment of capital, increases the assets of the firm, increases managerial complexity, and can cause loss of focus on core competencies. The reasons for investing in vertical integration go beyond the management of commodity price volatility, and are taken at the higher level of top management. Nevertheless, these decisions can be strongly influenced by the need to mitigate commodity price risk. For example, many oil companies such as ExxonMobile and

Royal Dutch Shell are vertically integrated owning upstream exploration and production and downstream refining. However, Marathon Petroleum and Marathon Oil, which were once vertically integrated, split into two companies: one focused on downstream refining, distribution, and retailing, and the other focused on upstream exploration and production. Considering these examples, we remember—once again—that "one size does not fit all."

Looking at the upstream supply chain, companies also may choose to buy from vertically integrated suppliers. An advantage of vertically integrated suppliers is that the supplier is not exposed to direct market pricing for its raw materials, reducing volatility and also does not pay for the supplier's margin. However, the choice of vertical integration is often more focused for supply assurance rather than as an approach for managing commodity price volatility.

Summary

This chapter provides a discussion of approaches and techniques that supply chain professionals can implement for managing price risk associated with value chain (supplier) commodity purchases. Similar to direct commodity purchases, there is "no one size fits all" approach for managing price fluctuations of value chain purchases. Firm size, supply management expertise, power in the supply chain, customer requirements, and a myriad of other factors influence the ability and availability of approaches for mitigating this risk. The approaches described in this chapter are provided in order of complexity or difficulty in implementation. The more complex processes are, generally, the more expensive or difficult to implement.

Section IV of this book will provide greater insights to the forecasting processes discussed with regard to technical and fundamental analysis in Chapters 3 and 4, and the commodity price risk management approaches examined in Chapters 5 and 6 by providing further details on several of the approaches previously discussed, as well as specific examples of how firms have created strategies in their organizations, supply chains, and environments in addressing commodity price volatility.

SECTION IV
Cases and Additional Observations

CHAPTER 7

Political Risk: The Case of Heavy Rare Earth Metals

Introduction

A myriad of risk sources amplify commodity price volatility, as discussed throughout this book. One specific case in point that we wish to elaborate more on concerns the influence of political risk. In today's global supply chains, firms increasingly interact with supply chain members in countries such as China, Russia, and Brazil, which to a high degree are either state-owned[1] or significantly influenced by national policy agendas.[2] We will discuss this source of risk given the recent example and developments occurring with heavy rare earth metals (HREM).

Understanding the Heavy Rare Earth Metals Market

The sourcing of HREM from China provides a particularly information-rich setting for four reasons.[3] First, the Western green-tech industry requires HREMs[4] in general and four HREMs in particular (europium, terbium, dysprosium, and yttrium) as mandatory inputs to their sustainability-focused business models of offering green-tech products, such as electrical/hybrid vehicles, solar collectors/photovoltaic systems, and wind turbines.[5] Second, the Western green-tech industry relies on Chinese HREM suppliers, which produce and control approximately 95 percent of the world's HREM supply.[6] Third, China's objective of reducing the high environmental burden from its formerly often illegally operated domestic HREM mining and refining firms caused it to consolidate its HREM industry under the state-owned Baotou Iron and Steel Group.[7] This consolidation effectively enabled China to control and eliminate the mining and refining capacity of illegally operated mines and refineries and to implement consistently higher environmental standards. Fourth, the state-owned Baotou Iron and Steel Group serves China as a vehicle to preserve its domestic green-tech industry, resulting in lower HREM mining and refining capacities.

Until 2009, the sourcing of HREMs posed few challenges to Western buying firms, and supply and price risks were not anticipated. This situation changed significantly in 2010 with the transition of China's HREM strategy. China's new domestic focus, combined with the reduced Chinese HREM export quotas and high export taxes, occurred at a time when world demand for rare earth metals rose in response to the growing demand for green-tech products.[8] This led to price surges and concerns about the future supply of HREMs outside China;[9] it also resulted in severe financial losses for the HREM-dependent Western green-tech industry as it sought to implement sustainability-focused business models.

How Firms Responded

These firms' strategies helped only partially to reduce the negative consequences from politically driven supply risk. The firms also realized that these initiatives still did not address the full set of root causes of HREM risk. They became aware that addressing these causes might require them to engage in activities beyond the buyer–supplier relationship and to reach out to additional entities in their networks. Based on this shift, some firms pursued a combination of commercial and technical mitigation strategies together with current and new members of their HREM supply chains (so called network-centric commercial and technical mitigation). For instance, one wind turbine manufacturer and its battery component supplier invested in the capital-intensive development of a magnet joint venture (JV), together with an international mining firm (third party) as a means to develop a second source strategy for HREMs. As part of this JV, the mining firm contributes its technical HREM mining knowledge and guarantees that it will deliver all mined HREMs exclusively to the manufacturer and its supplier; the battery supplier contributes its technical knowledge of how to produce magnets from HREM powders; and the wind turbine manufacturer and its battery supplier commercially guarantee their purchase of magnets exclusively from the magnet JV (through a multi-year off-take agreement). This JV corresponds to backward vertical integration of the manufacturer and its supplier into the upstream mining sector and forward vertical integration of the international mining firm into the downstream manufacturing of magnets.

In another case, two component suppliers from the luminescence industry, together with several recycling firms, invested in a recycling program for luminescence products. As part of this cooperation, the recycling firms provided their technical capabilities in separating HREMs from returned luminescence products, and the two suppliers commercially guaranteed an HREM buyback quota at below-HREM market prices to the recycling firms. As a result, these firms could regain HREMs from recycled end products and therefore reduce their dependence on Chinese HREMs.

In addition, when Western green-tech firms fully realized that HREM price and availability uncertainties were, for the foreseeable future, significantly controlled by the national Chinese policy agenda, they also began putting the HREM issue on the agenda of political decision makers in their home countries. Although the firms were cognizant of the political causes of the HREM supply risk, many firms actively engaged in political agenda setting. Along the same lines, in some companies board members started discussing their industry's rare earth metal dependence on China with the government and politicians, including an exchange with the national Ministry of Economics and Energy. Furthermore, firms joined cross-firm alliances to actively engage in political activities, such as bundling resource-related firm interests and connecting with influential politicians who can represent the allied firms' and their own nations' interests in the security of natural resources. Examples of such alliances include a U.S. alliance—Rare Earth Technology Alliance (RETA); a Japanese alliance—Japan Oil, Gas, and Metals National Corporation (JOGMEC); a French alliance—Comité pour les Métaux Stratégiques (COMES); and a German alliance—Allianz zur Rohstoffsicherung (ARC). Firms use these vehicles to garner political support to secure access to critical resources, such as HREMs, nonferrous metals (e.g., copper, aluminum), specialty metals (e.g., lithium, cobalt), coal, and graphite in foreign countries. One illustration of the potential influence of such alliances includes political visits to China, Mongolia, and Kazakhstan by German Chancellor Angela Merkel, during which she represented German firms' resource interests, including HREMs.[10] The multicountry-initiated World Trade Organization (WTO) dispute and associated ruling against China's HREM export politics in early 2014[11] and the ending of the export quotas by China in early 2015[12] also illustrate how effective such alliances can be.

This shows that the basic assumption underlying today's supply chains—namely, that the interaction in supply chains is among private firms coordinated through basic market mechanisms and supply chain members' mutual commitment and trust[13] is being challenged by contemporary supply chain realities. In addition to rare earth metals, other critical raw materials—such as specialty metals (e.g., lithium, antimony, cobalt, molybdenum, tungsten), nonferrous metals (e.g., copper, aluminum, zinc, tin, lead), and semimetal graphite—are mostly extracted and processed in geopolitically unstable regions and countries that follow state-promoted export policies.[14] As North American and European countries increasingly import these critical raw materials, Western firms likely will encounter further politically motivated interests in international supply markets and the resulting structural imbalances, disruptions, or conflicts, in which state-owned suppliers have little motivation to withhold the exercise of their power.

Practical Approaches for Managing Political Risk

This has several important practical implications. First, existing supply market intelligence systems and models might need to be upgraded to more fully and quickly capture, for example, increasingly important political influences on supply chains and to simulate their effects. Second, supply managers who face political supply risk might consider active engagement in coalitions (e.g., the formation of alliances within and across supply chains) with other supply chain partners facing the same or similar risk. Managers need to be aware that actors—such as national governments enforcing state-promoted interests on international supply markets—might become more a norm than an exception. Third, to effectively mitigate political supply risk, managers might want to consider refining and expanding their existing repertoire of knowledge and skills. This need for such expansion seems particularly pronounced when risk is high—when the respective raw materials are both critical and scarce.

Fourth, although the current networks of purchasing managers mainly target finding and exchanging commercial and technical best practices, the effective mitigation of political supply risk appears to require a broadened scope for related initiatives. Specifically, chief purchasing officers (CPOs) might therefore want to cast a wider net in terms of assessing politically induced risk and reaching out to partners in their mitigation efforts. Advancing and using both their business and political acumen should enable supply chain managers to strategically navigate increasingly complex supply chain contexts.

Both an extended coverage and reach of mitigation efforts and a quick shift from one mode of operation to another seem to be more feasible for firms when they are facilitated by an even stronger formal and informal strategic integration of the supply chain management (SCM)/purchasing function. Top management should then ensure that SCM/purchasing has formal channels (i.e., representation on key committees) to access decision makers and to escalate any topics of strategic importance without delay. SCM/purchasing managers might also want to ensure open, informal, firm-internal channels. When the SCM/purchasing function has a strong internal reputation as a business partner for line management, its managers have easier access to the full range of strategic and general management functions when needed.

The HREM case also demonstrates that it is highly important for buying firms to be able to trace the provenance of their inputs at all stages of the supply chain. This is true not only for HREM. Traceability is a critical prerequisite for managing commodity price risk management and is the widely covered case of "conflict minerals" (CM)—tin, tantalum, tungsten, and gold—which are mined in the Democratic Republic of the Congo (DRC) and, after being smelted, are being used mainly in consumer electronics products, such as mobile phones and computers. Armed groups in the DRC earn large amounts of money by mining and trading CM, and in that process they continually violate the most basic human rights. To end the trade in CM, the U.S. Dodd-Frank Act (DFA) has recently forced listed companies to determine whether any of their products contain CM. Since individual firms are required to trace the provenance of the minerals, this regulation forces them to map their entire supply chain. Related to this example, recent allegations by consumers and nongovernmental organizations (NGOs) suggest that companies in the electronics and automobile sectors support child labor through their sourcing of raw materials or companies in the food and retail industries support slave labor in the fishing sector or the garment industry[15] underscore the relevance of understanding traceability for addressing social issues.

Summary

Complex, global supply chains require companies (a) to trace the provenance of their inputs at all stages of the supply chain, and (b) to understand, anticipate, influence, and respond to political influences in their supply chains. HREMs provide one example of this risk. As we have discussed in the case of HREMs, commodity price volatility is one manifestation of political risk, with others including, but are not limited to, threats of supply disruptions, environmental and social sustainability effects. Supply chain professionals, in their management of global supply chains, need to be strategic, with the "buy-in" of other business functions and supply chain and industry partners, to holistically manage political risk. These efforts are critical for creating sustainable and resilient firms and supply chains in an ever-complex environment.

CHAPTER 8

Using Commodities as Collateral: The Case of China

Antonio Cesarano

Head of Market Strategy, MPS CAPITAL SERVICES

Background

In recent years, commodity prices have experienced significant fluctuations, with different reactions from financial markets. In particular, the dynamics of commodity prices showed significant differences during the economic and financial crisis that began in September 2008 (i.e., the month of the default of the former government-sponsored enterprises (GSEs) Fannie Mae and Freddie Mac). In response, in the following months, the U.S. Federal Reserve (FED) spent billions to buy back Treasury notes and mortgage-backed securities. During the two years after the crisis began, the U.S. government was forced to create the TARP (Troubled Asset Relief Program) fund to recapitalize banks. In fact, the first two years of the crisis were characterized by a strong correlation between injections of liquidity by Central Banks and the resulting sharp increases in raw materials. This dynamic is the result stemming from several other factors.

The *strong monetary expansion* practiced—predominantly—by the U.S. Central Bank had increased the expectation of a rapid recovery of the world's largest economy. Consequently, it also increased the expectations of the recovery of the Chinese economy, which, in turn, was highly dependent on the U.S. demand. This aspect appears to be particularly relevant. In fact, in the years before the financial crisis, China was among the main consumers in the world of many different commodities. Therefore, when supporting the U.S. growth, the FED expansionary policies indirectly supported the Chinese economy, increasing the expectation of a strong growth in demand for commodities.

Besides these dynamics, the financial market reacted by generating *strong price fluctuations* and high volatility conditions, especially if compared with the precrisis phase, as we can see from Figures 8.1 and 8.2.

We refer here not only to the speculative component, but also to the stronger presence of some institutional investors, characterized by interests in long-term investments. This was the case of pension funds investors, which, in that period, increased the exposure of this asset class, with

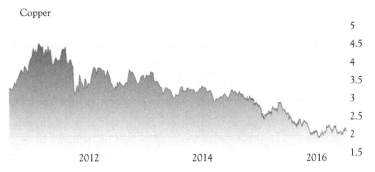

Figure 8.1 Copper price fluctuation between 2007 and 2016

Source: Trading economics.[1]

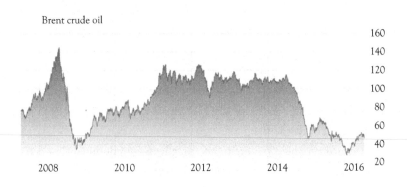

Figure 8.2 Brent crude oil price fluctuation between 2007 and 2016

Source: Trading economics.[2]

different purposes. First was the chance to take advantage of the increase in global demand, increasing the performance of their portfolios. Moreover, commodities appeared to be an asset potentially capable to "hedge" against the risk of higher inflation and market rates, driven by monetary policies.

However, since 2010 the situation changed. In fact, raw material price dynamics started experiencing minor fluctuations. During the second phase of the crisis the Euro-zone suffered much more than other regions. The beginning can be traced back to the default of Greece in mid-2010, followed by similar cases in Portugal and Ireland, with a subsequent wide and deep spread to Italy. In this phase there were the first signs of a slow-down in the Chinese economy, with the simultaneous gradual downsizing of the global demand for commodities. Despite further monetary policies on a global scale, in this situation commodity prices did increase. Speculation did not find the support of the demand increase for Chinese commodities anymore, which was relevant during 2008 to 2010. Moreover, major central banks expressed an explicit commitment in maintaining low interest rates, allowing a gradual increase of pure carry trade deals. Further the financial markets have increasingly preferred bonds carry trades, rather than directional trades in the commodity market.

The downsizing of Chinese demand, and the resulting major stability of the main commodities (with respect to the first 2 years of the crisis), has gradually reduced commodity price risk perceptions. Consequently, companies reduced the demand for hedging products. In addition, higher regulatory constraints have been imposed to the world's leading brokers, with consequent higher trading costs for commodities. Many financial operators, which had introduced and/or increased the weight of commodities in their asset allocation, changed strategies. Moreover, investors perceived that the risk of disinflation/deflation was significantly higher than commodity price risk. All these factors influenced a global reduction of the commodities trading.

In the context of declining interest rates, some financial institutions started considering asset liability management (ALM) investments. This is the case of pension funds, for which the aging population trend leads to an increase in the pensions to be paid. At the same time, the strong and rapid decline in market interest rates resulted in an equally sharp decline in asset yields, boosting the issues of risk from an ALM perspective. Consequently, some pension funds have begun to downsize the total return portfolio assets, which were able to generate good performances in terms of capital gains. This downsizing has most likely affected commodity markets. This was maybe due to the expected low performance—in terms of flows—linked to commodities.

The Use of Commodities as Collateral

In recent years the use of commodities as collateral to obtain loans has increased. The phenomenon has spread particularly in China and has concerned mainly industrial raw materials (in particular copper, aluminum, iron, and gold) because of their characteristic of being nonperishable. Some analysts estimate the amount of foreign exchange loans in China with commodities as collateral to be about $109 billion. This amount is equal to the 31 percent of total Chinese short-term currency loans, and the 14 percent of all foreign currency loans regardless of maturity.[3]

This phenomenon (so-called commodity-based financing) has become a crucial driver of shadow banking in China. It is a kind of parallel system of funding for Chinese companies, in addition to traditional banking. According to an analysis produced by ANZ bank, the assets in the hands of "shadow banks" reached about $4,900 billion, representing approximately 50 percent of the country's gross domestic product (GDP).[4] The most common form of "shadow banking" is represented by the "Trust companies" that are companies specialized in investing in sectors with high potential returns. As reported by the China Trustee Association, the assets managed were the equivalent of about $2,500 billion at the end of December 2015, a 16.6 percent over the same period in 2014.

A typical scheme for connecting commodity-financing to Chinese trusts includes the following main steps:

1. A Chinese company (A) specialized in import–export subscribes a commodities purchase contract with a foreign company.
2. The same company (A) uses the commodities purchase contract to request a credit note (with maturities typically between 3 to 6 months) to a domestic or foreign bank. The loan is in U.S. dollars, the currency needed to pay for commodities. To get the credit, the

Chinese importing company will have to pay a margin, generally between 20 and 30 percent of the total loan. In turn, the importer may sell futures on Chinese markets to protect itself from the risk of a decline in commodity prices.

3. Commodities are shipped to storage sites located in China (usually adjacent to the ports). The importing company receives a certificate attesting the arrival of the commodities by the storage site operator.

4. With this certificate the company (A) goes to a domestic bank to obtain loans in yuan, offering the deposited commodities as guarantee. The bank grants the loan in yuan, typically applying a fee (the so-called haircut) of around 30 percent, which means a lower rate than in the case of absence or other guarantee.

5. The company (A) invests the loan in yuan by offering the borrowed funds to small organizations operating in high growth sectors. Often the investment is made through the purchasing of trust units. Therefore, by the expiring date, the company (A) will gain the differential between the low cost of funding in yuan (thanks to the collateralization effect offered by commodities) and the high expected returns from investments. Figure 8.3 represents a typical process of commodity-based financing.

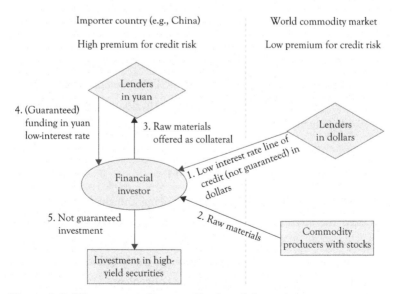

Figure 8.3 The process of commodity-based financing

Source: Commodities as collateral.[5]

Sectors that represent typical investment destinations are those in the composition of the assets of the Chinese trust, as shown by the China Trustee Association. At the end of June 2014, 50 percent was invested in industrial companies and infrastructure industry, and about 11 percent in the real estate sector. One of the fundamental points of a commodity-financing scheme is the presence of a low level of the Libor rate in U.S. dollar compared to Shibor rate.[6]

The close connection between the world of Chinese trusts and the trend of commodities used in commodity-financing has been evident during 2014. Two have been the most striking episodes.

- On March 5, 2014, a Chinese company producing solar panels (the Shanghai Chaori Solar) declared it was not able to pay interests of about $15 million on some bonds near to maturity. After this announcement, copper recorded a decline of about 9 percent in a week. It was the first default on Chinese corporate bonds, which increased the perception that the phenomenon could be more widespread. The default could have probably led the domestic financing bank to use the collateral for the loan offered in yuan, in this case leading to a sharp decline in the copper price.[7]
- On June 4, 2014, an ongoing investigation by the Chinese authorities was reported about port of Qingdao—offering copper as collateral for various loans. An investigation was opened after a complaint made by CITIC Resources Holdings Limited (one of China's most important financial companies publicly owned).

Summary

The strong link between commodity financing and shadow banking has attracted the attention of the government that is trying to curb these transactions. At the beginning of Chinese Lunar New Year of 2014, there has been a marked depreciation of the yuan, partly induced just to make investments in commodity financing less convenient.

From the aforesaid considerations, the attempt to control the phenomenon (already partially evident from the abovementioned sharp decline in growth of the assets of the Chinese trusts) turns out to be critical. There are—in particular—some potential consequences in terms of credit reduction to small–medium Chinese companies, and in terms of new price reduction trends, similar to the dynamics of 2014.

This chapter started describing what recently happened in the financial market, particularly after the crisis of 2008 and the FED's reaction. Since 2010 the situation has changed, and the use of commodities as collateral to obtain loans has increased. In particular, the chapter aimed at describing how this phenomenon has spread, particularly in China, and has involved mainly industrial raw materials. In parallel, during the last years, the Chinese economic slowdown caused a general reduction of the global commodities' demand, strongly influencing commodity prices. Looking at the future, we expect that two drivers will determine the commodity price volatility: the Chinese market dynamic and the use of commodities for financial speculation.

CHAPTER 9

Further Insights on Financial Hedging Instruments

Ugo Montagnini

Corporate Sales–Customer Desk Corporate,
MPS CAPITAL SERVICES

Background

A hedge is a financial investment used to reduce the risk of unfavorable price movements in an asset. A hedge typically means taking an offsetting position in a related security, such as a futures contract when you will be buying or selling an asset, such as a commodity, in the future. For example, a farmer who will sell wheat in the future can hedge by buying a futures contract now then selling that contract at a future date. Financial tools that can be used are derivatives, which typically move in parallel with the underlying asset: they include options, swaps, futures and forward contracts. These derivatives are only financial instruments and are not related to the underlying assets. The underlying assets can be commodities, but also—in a broader perspective—stocks, bonds, currencies, indices, or interest rates. The derivatives are typically traded on organized exchanges but in some cases banks act as intermediaries for trading of derivatives.

It is essential to know how to make decisions about financial hedging in order to assure reliability and effectiveness to the financial coverage. In particular, there are three conditions that determine whether to pursue a hedging strategy:

- The presence of a financial market where the commodity is listed.

- The time horizon in the financial market, in terms of quotations "bid/ask."
- The liquidity in each time frame, in terms of volume of contracts (open interest).

When making decisions about financial hedging for managing commodity price volatility, these conditions are essential, because for commodities, the financial markets often are not liquid and are influenced by several exogenous factors. In case of liquid markets, the bid/ask spread is narrow and the price of the physical commodity is similar to the quotation available on the financial market. An example of a very liquid market is the London Metal Exchange (LME), where the following underlying assets are listed: high-grade aluminum, aluminum alloy, NASAAC (North American Special Aluminum Alloy Contract), copper, lead, nickel, tin, zinc, and steel rods. The LME is the world's leading market for industrial metals, with over 80 percent of metals contracts traded in this market. In this case, the quotations of the financial market are taken as the basis to determine the price at which the contracts will be negotiated for the physical exchange between customers and suppliers.

Table 9.1 highlights a list of commodities on which it is possible to apply financial hedging; the list is just an example, because the "world of hedging" on commodities is continuously evolving.

However, not all commodities can be effectively hedged. In presence of "oligopolies," futures often show non-relevant open interests, high bid/ask spreads, as well as short time horizons. These factors result in a mismatch between the physical price (that is paid for the supply of the physical assets) and the financial derivative quotation. In oligopoly markets, such as in the steel market, price and quantities are determined by a few players. This generates a substantial lack of supply/demand in the financial market. In 2005, for example, there was an attempt to list—for the first time—futures contracts for plastic materials (polyethylene and polypropylene) on LME. However, due to the lack of liquidity, these products were removed in 2011.

In case of commodities not directly listed on financial markets, such as semifinished materials, it is still possible to cross-hedge by doing a correlation study between the underlying asset (historical prices of commodities)

Table 9.1 Example of financial derivatives

Precious metals	Exchange	Location
Gold	NYMEX-IPE	New York–London
Silver	COMEX	New York
Platinum	NYMEX	New York
Palladium	NYMEX	New York
Industrial metals	**Exchange**	**Location**
Aluminum high grade	LME	London
Aluminum alloy	LME	London
Copper	LME	London
Zinc	LME	London
Lead	LME	London
Nickel	LME	London
Pond	LME	London
Steel	LME	London
Energy	**Exchange**	**Location**
WTI oil	NYMEX-IPE	New York–London
Brent oil	IPE	London
Naphtha	Platts	London
Diesel fuel	NYMEX	New York
Heating oil	NYMEX	New York
Natural gas	NYMEX	New York
Gas formulas	Platts	London
Formulas electricity	Platts	London
Agriculture	**Exchange**	**Location**
Wheat	CBT/Euronext	Chicago–Parigi
Corn	CBT/Euronext	Chicago–Parigi
Soybeans	CBT	Chicago
Rapeseed	Euronext	Parigi
Soft	**Exchange**	**Location**
Arabica coffee	NYBOT	New York
Robusta coffee	LIFFE	London
Brown sugar	NYBOT	New York
White sugar	LIFFE	London
Cotton	NYBOT	New York

and identifying specific indexes/markets whose movements are correlated with the underlying asset. Cross-hedging is used in a number of situations, for example, feed for livestock manufacturers, confectionery companies, and for companies using oil derivatives.

Another condition that influences the ability to financially hedge is firm size. Large corporations, characterized with average volume of annual sales exceeding $500 million typically have the resources to manage commodity risk, and can use financial hedging in a structured way to optimize their operating results. Medium-sized companies, with average annual sales between $100 million and $500 million, often have structured organizational charts that allow an effective management of commodity risk and the adoption of hedging strategies, with formal coop-eration between the purchasing manager/buyer and the chief financial officer (CFO). In smaller firms, with average sales less than $100 million, purchases are generally under the responsibility of the chief executive officer (CEO), and the use of financial derivatives for hedging is limited.

Hedging Structures

If the conditions favor hedging, there are various hedging structures that organizations can employ to implement hedging. The hedging structures are typically divided into two categories, depending on the level of standardization and there are a number of approaches that can be used in each. Here we describe "Plain Vanilla" and "Non-Plain Vanilla" approaches from the buyer's perspective. Additional explanations and descriptions of the following terms in these structures can be found in Kolb and Overdahl[1] and Schofield.[2]

Plain Vanilla Structures

Here we describe four different "Plain Vanilla" approaches, presenting advantages and risks of each of them. Purchasing organizations can decide to hedge using the so-called "calls and puts" options financial derivatives. Options are used to hedge the risk of commodity price increases. A call option gives the buyer the right to buy a specific amount of an asset any time before the expiration of the option but the buyer is not required to make the purchase. A call option is similar but in this case the right is to sell a specific amount of the underlying commodity rather than to buy it. The buyer of an asset who is exposed to the risk of commodity price increases has financial protection against an adverse price movement by purchasing a call option. This instrument requires the payment of an initial premium.

The main advantages of the "calls and puts" options are the following:

- The buyer is able to predetermine the maximum purchasing cost.
- The buyer, in the case of a commodity price decrease, does not have to exercise the option, losing only the purchase price of the option and can buy the commodity at the market price.

The main risks of the "calls and puts" options are the following:

- The option has an initial cost that will not necessarily be offset by a positive revenue.
- In the event of an early resolution, the market value may be lower than the premium paid at the time of the contract; in this case, the customer will lose part of the value paid for the financial tool.
- If the commodity price decreases, the customer can't receive the corresponding gain since the "calls and puts" option aims only to assure a financial protection against adverse price movements.

Another financial derivative is the so-called "Asian calls and puts" option. This is a financial instrument that requires the payment of a premium, allowing the buyer of the commodity to protect itself against upward fluctuations in the commodity price, and providing in advance the maximum value of purchase on average, without additional obligations in case of adverse movements in the commodity market. The difference from other "calls and puts" options lies in the mechanism for the pay-off calculation. The pay-off for "Asian calls and puts" options is based on an average price of the commodity, determined in a predefined period of time, while for the other "calls and puts" tools the pay-off of the option is related to the price of the commodity within an exercise.

The main advantages of the "Asian calls and puts" option are the following:

- The buyer is able to predetermine the maximum purchasing cost.
- The buyer, in the case of a commodity price decrease, may leave the option and buy the commodity at the market price.

The main risks of the "Asian calls and puts" option are the following:

- The option has an initial cost that will not necessarily be offset by positive revenue.
- In the event of an early resolution, the market value may be lower than the premium paid at the time of the contract.
- If the commodity price decreases, the customer will never see a positive spread.

A third plain vanilla structure is the so-called synthetics forward contracts (SFCs). This is a hedging instrument that allows the buyers of commodities to protect themselves against upward fluctuations in the price of a commodity for a specific time frame. In this case, there is the purchase of a call option and the concurrent selling of a put option at the same strike price and the same notional amount on a specific underlying asset and on a specific date. The investor typically combines long calls and short puts. In order to have a position that is similar to a regular forward contract, the call option and the put option have the same strike price and expiration date. The investor pays a "net option premium" when executing a synthetic forward contract, but part of the long position cost is offset by the short position. This strategy enables the customer to set a predetermined purchasing price of the underlying asset.

The main advantage of the "SFC contract" is the following:

- The buyer is able to predetermine a certain purchasing price, and therefore there is a real protection in case of price increase.

The main risks of the "SFC contract" are the following:

- In the case of an early resolution, should the movement of the underlying asset price be opposite to the position taken by the customer, the buyer may pay an amount, which is not quantifiable *ex ante* in the form of market value.
- The product does not allow the buyer to benefit from a favorable movement of the underlying asset price.

A fourth tool is the "Commodity swap." This is a contract in which the underlying asset is a commodity, whose amount is determined by the most commonly used parameter (e.g., markets' standard cubic meters, bbl, lb, m/ton). The contract requires the payment of a fixed price by the customer, agreed between the parties. At the same time, the customer receives the amount given at a variable price, determined on the basis of defined parameters or calculated by a formula linked to the future cost of commodities and agreed by the parties. At the end of each period (monthly, bimonthly, quarterly, half-yearly), two different scenarios may occur, linked to the cost emerging between two specific dates. In the first scenario, the variable price is higher than the fixed price: the counterparty who paid the variable price (the bank) will provide the positive spread between the variable price and the fixed price, multiplied by the quantity of the commodity in the period of reference. In the second scenario, the variable price is lower than the fixed price: the counterparty who paid the fixed price (the customer) will provide the positive difference between the fixed price and variable price, multiplied by the quantity of the commodity in the period of reference.

The main advantages of the "commodity swap" are the following:

- The buyer knows in advance the maximum purchasing cost.
- The buyer is protected against the commodity price increase.

The main risks of the "commodity swap" are the following:

- The contract does not allow the buyer to benefit from a downward movement of the price.
- In the event of an early resolution, should the price move downward, the buyer may pay an amount not quantifiable *ex ante* in the form of market value.

Non-Plain Vanilla Structures

In this section we describe three different "Non-Plain Vanilla" approaches, SFCs with knock-in (KI), collar, and collar with KI, and present the advantages and risks of each of them.

The SFCs with KI are hedging instruments that allow the buyer of a commodity to be protected against upward fluctuations of the commodity price covered by the agreement on a set date. This tool gives the opportunity to benefit from a depreciation of the commodity up to a predetermined level (barrier level) for improvement of price movements compared to the barrier level the buyer buys its raw materials at the agreed strike price. This involves the purchase of a call option and the sale of a "knock in" (trigger barrier) put option at the same strike price and the same notional amount on a specific underlying asset and on a specific date. The strategy enables the buyer to set a predetermined purchasing price. Being a customized product, the duration is determined by the buyer and usually the option's expiration is aligned with the expiration of the payment set in the contract.

The main advantages of the "SFC with KI" are the following:

- Buyer predetermines a certain purchase price of the commodity and therefore is protected from the price increase.

- The buyer can benefit from a favorable movement in the commodity price up to the lower barrier level.

The main risks of the "SFC with KI" are the following:

- In the event of an early resolution, should the movement of the price be opposite to the position taken by the customer, the buyer may pay an amount that is not quantifiable *ex ante* in the form of market value.
- The product does not allow the buyer to benefit from a favorable price movement (downward in the case of a customer buying commodity) for improvement levels up to the trigger barrier.

A second approach is the "Collar," a hedging product that allows the buyer of a commodity to be protected against upward fluctuations of the commodity price covered by the agreement on a set date, taking the opportunity of a more favorable price, up to a minimum level set in advance. The strategy consists of buying a call option at a certain level of strike price (upper limit) and, at the same time, selling a put option with a lower strike price (lower limit) than one of the purchased call option for the same notional amount on a specific underlying asset and a specific expiration date. The strategy enables the buyer to set a maximum purchasing price of the chosen underlying (strike of the purchased call option) with the possibility to benefit from a downward movement of the price up to a minimum price limit (strike put option sold). Being a customized product, the buyer determines the duration and usually the option's expiration coincides with the expiration of the payment set in the contract (beyond 24 months the market is nonliquid, and it is difficult to find efficient hedging instruments).

The main advantages of the "Collar" are the following:

- The buyer predetermines a certain purchasing price, assuring the protection from a price increase. At the same time the organization may benefit from a favorable movement in the price up to the strike level.

The main risks of the "Collar" are the following:

- In the event of an early resolution, should the movement of the price be opposite to the position taken by the buyer, the buyer may pay an amount that is not quantifiable *ex ante* in the form of market value.
- The product does not allow the buyer to benefit from a favorable movement of the price.

Different from the collar, is the so-called "Collar with Knock In," a hedging product involving a combination of different options: a CAP and a FLOOR, with a KNOCK-IN on the CAP. This allows you to be protected against upward fluctuations of the price of the commodity covered by the agreement on a set date, with the opportunity to benefit from a depreciation of the commodity cost up to a predetermined minimum level (barrier level). The strategy consists of buying a call option at a certain level of strike price (upper limit), selling—at the same time—a put option with a lower strike price (lower limit) than the one of the purchased call option for the same notional amount on a specific underlying asset and a specific expiration date. The strategy enables the customer to set a maximum purchasing price (strike of the purchased call option) with the possibility to benefit from a downward movement of the price up to a minimum price limit (strike put option sold). Being a customized product, the buyer determines the duration and usually the option's expiration is aligned with the expiration of the payment fixed in the contract (beyond 24 months the market is nonliquid, and it is difficult to find efficient hedging instruments).

The main advantage of the "Collar with Knock-In" is the following:

- The buyer predetermines a certain purchase price of the commodity; therefore there is a protection from the price increase. At the same time the organization may benefit from a favorable movement in the price up to the trigger barrier level.

The main risks of the "Collar with Knock-In" are the following:

- In the case of an early resolution, should the movement of the price be opposite to the position taken by the customer, the customer may pay an amount not quantifiable *ex ante* in the form of market value.
- The product does not allow the buyer to benefit from a favorable movement of the underlying price (downward in the case of the buyer) for better levels as to the barrier limit.

Examples of Hedging and Related Markets

Among the described hedging approaches, the most adopted one is the commodity swap. The contract requires the swap of a fixed price, agreed between the parties and expressed in the currency of reference per unit of goods, against a variable price (depending on the future value of the commodity) to certain fixed dates.

The fixed price of the swap is calculated as the sum of future cash flows discounted to the present.

We here analyze in detail the structure of financial flows related to a standard commodity swap where the swap premium is expressed in the same currency of the underlying commodity.

Be $T_1^F, ..., T_P^F$ a payment time series and $t_i^1, ..., t_i^{k_i}$ with $i = 1, ..., P$ a sample time series within any payment period. The exchanged cash flow at every payment time T_i^P is determined as follows:

$$Flow_i = \text{Nominal} * \left[\frac{\sum_{j=1}^{k_i} C(t_i^j)}{k_i} - K \right]$$

where $C(t_i^j)$ is the value of the commodity underlying the swap at the time t_i^j and K the strike (fixed price) of the swap.

If the premium for the swap is expressed in a different currency from the currency of the underlying commodity we adjust the formula

$$Flow_i = \text{Nominal} * \left[\frac{\sum_{j=1}^{k_i} C(t_i^j) * Fx(t_i^j)}{k_i} - K \right]$$

where $Fx(t_i^j)$ represents the exchange rate foreign currency/premium currency to the time t_i^j.

Thus, in the multicurrency swaps, the variable exchange rate is included in order to determine the pay-off. Obviously this variable will be analyzed and managed during the life of the swap product.

Example 1

This example describes a cost-risk commodity swap whose underlying is the contract of a future (first nearby futures) on Brent Crude Oil listed on the Intercontinental Exchange (ICE) platform:

- Pricing date: 05/31/2016
- Start date: 10/01/2016
- Expiry date: 10/31/2016
- Payment date: 11/15/2016
- Fixing dates: Every business day from 10/01/2016 to 10/31/2016 included
- Volumes: 10,000 barrels
- Strike (fixed price): 51.90 USD/bbl (dollars per barrel)
- Customer pays fixed price
- Customer receives variable price (=arithmetic monthly average of the fixing in October 2016 of the first nearby futures on Brent).

In order to determine the swap strike (fixed price) it is necessary to identify the futures and the related lot on the "market" that identify the underlying.

Levels of the future detected on the ICE platform to the pricing date:

Future December 16th, expiration date 10/31/16, 51.90 USD/bbl

In this example the customer's financial position is "long," and thus will benefit from the structure in the case of an appreciation of the Brent during the life of the swap. The position of the bank that has quoted the swap will conversely be "short." The cash flow swap traded at the payment time will be determined as: (arithmetic mean of the official closing prices of the first nearby futures reported within the period of observation – strike price) * volume.

In the specific case, as we will see in the following, it is interesting to investigate the use of the arithmetic mean to determine the variable flows of the swap for the correct analysis of the risk profile of the product itself and the relative hedging. The fixing of the commodity, on a daily observation, becomes a deterministic component in calculating the arithmetical mean.

Considering 21 working days in the month of October, on October 3rd, our instrument will present an already determined observation and 20 residual observations of component "variable/risky" up to the maturity. At this point, the bank defines the strike, and then builds up the hedge position.

Recalling that the volumes shown in the example is 10,000 barrels, and that a single contract (lot) of futures on Brent is equivalent to a volume of 1,000 barrels, the alternatives to the intermediary are as follows:

1. The bank goes on the over-the-counter (OTC) market, where swaps on the Brent are actively traded on. The commodity swap contracts on Brent are very "liquid," that means they present very narrow bid/offer spreads and with significant volumes of a wide spectrum of maturities. In this case the bank that sold the swap to the customer buys it again on the OTC market to volumes equal to 10,000 barrels. The structure of financial flows of the swap closed with the market is perfectly aligned and coinciding with the transaction executed with the customer.

2. The bank operates on the futures market, purchasing 10 lots of futures (equivalent to 10,000 barrels) of Brent expiring on December 16th. In this case the profile of the swap cash flows is replicated with the reference futures. Once the swap has daily observations (fixings), and then the calculation of the average becomes the expression of a

deterministic component and of a variable, the hedging strategy will have to be updated by selling those lots of futures that are in "excess" compared with the new swap risk profile.

Example 2

Now we consider the case in which the underlying commodity of the swap is a "distilled oil" (i.e., gasoline, diesel, fuel) meaning it is a product that comes from the refining process of the oil and that presents some OTC markets, which are less liquid than the Brent market.

We assume that the first reference commodity of the swap is the Fuel Oil 1 percent CIF MED. The acronyms CIF and FOB specify whether the naval cargo transportation of the oil includes or not the cost of insurance, shipping, and other related costs (CIF: Cost, Insurance, and Freight – FOB: Free on Board), while the acronym MED specifies that the delivery will be at the Mediterranean ports.

The daily values of the Fuel Oil and many other oil derivatives are determined through a daily survey of the main operators of the sector carried out by specialized agencies (information providers) such as Platts or Argus. The values determined in this way represent the daily observations (fixings) that will determine the swap pay-off. Therefore, in this second example, the underlying on which to perform the swap hedging will not be the first nearby future as for the Brent but a spot value determined by using data provided by an information provider.

- Pricing date: 05/31/2016
- Start date: 10/01/2016
- Expiry date: 10/31/2016
- Payment dates: 15/11/2016
- Fixing dates: Every business day from 10/01/2016 to 10/31/2016 included
- Volume: 1,000 MT (metric tons)
- Strike: 257.00 USD/MT
- Customer pays fixed price
- Customer receives variable price (=arithmetic monthly average of the fixing in October 2016).

Being Fuel Oil 1 percent CIF MED is an oil derivative, the swaps on this commodity has a quotation price that is a direct function of the swap price on Brent plus a spread (called crack spread). The term *crack spreads* is related to the name of the process by which the fuel oil is created from crude oil: the cracking process.

The levels of crack spreads and swaps on the OTC Brent detected to the pricing time are:

- Crack spread, 10/31/2016 expiration date – 11.427 USD/bbl
- Swaps on Crude Oil Brent, 10/31/2016 expiration date, 51.90 USD/bbl
- Calculation of the strike:
  Strike = (51.90 – 11.427) × 6.35 = 257.00 USD/MT

The value 6.35 expresses the standard conversion on financial markets to convert barrels in metric ton. In the aforementioned example, a volume of 1,000 MT is equivalent to 6,350 bbls. In this example the customer's financial position is "long," so they will have a benefit from the structure in the case of an appreciation of the Fuel Oil during the life of the swap. Conversely, the position of the bank has quoted the swap will be "short."

Once agreed the strike and improved the operation, the bank builds up the hedge position. This is done by the purchasing of the crack spread on the market using the following combination of commodity swaps:

- Purchasing commodity swaps with underlying Fuel Oil 1 percent CIF MED, 1,000 MT volume. This position perfectly covers the exposure of the intermediary toward the customer.
- Selling commodity swaps with underlying Brent Crude Oil, 6,350 bbls volume.

This last open position on Brent can be covered by:

- Purchasing on the OTC market an underlying commodity Brent Crude Oil swap.
- Managing the swap risk with futures listed on the ICE platform (as seen in the previous example).

The intermediary, in this case, has changed its position from an exposure to an extremely "inefficient/illiquid" underlying, such as the Fuel Oil, to a risk position linked to the very liquid Crude Oil.

Summary

In this chapter, we briefly described the most used hedging structures that companies can adopt in order to mitigate commodity price risk. We also described the "best conditions" that organizations should face in order to invest on efficient and effective financial hedging approaches.

The social, economic, and competitive environment is rapidly changing, and commodity price volatility is generally increasing. For these reasons organizations are paying increasing attention to commodity price risk mitigation and financial hedging approaches. On the other side, financial institutions and banks are proposing innovative solutions in order to better help companies manage risk. From the market perspective, we observe that financial markets will become more liquid and dynamic in the future, and there will be an increasing number of raw materials that could be hedged using financial derivatives. A challenge is to increase information exchange and transparency in these markets. From the industry's perspective, organizations should develop competences and skills in their purchasing offices in order to better manage the procurement of price volatile raw materials.

Notes

Preface

1. Zsidisin et al. (2014).
2. Zsidisin, Hartley, and Kaufmann (2013).
3. Gaudenzi et al. (2015).
4. Zsidisin et al. (2014).

Chapter 1

1. Brown, Crawford, and Gibson (2008).
2. Brown, Crawford, and Gibson (2008).
3. Trading Economics (2016).
4. Christian (2011).
5. The Silver Institute (2011).
6. Kellogg's 2010 Annual Report (2010, 6).
7. Tseng (2011).
8. Skybus Airlines to Cease Operations (2008).
9. Martin (2011).
10. Web Tool: Strategic Profit Model (n.d.).
11. Reed (2008).
12. Turner and Lim (2015).
13. CORDIS (n.d.).
14. Clifford (2011).

Chapter 2

1. Pandit and Marmanis (2008).
2. Zsidisin (2005).
3. Henry Hub Natural Gas Futures (n.d.).
4. Natural Gas Spot and Futures Prices (NYMEX) (n.d.).
5. Natural Gas Prices (2016).
6. Natural Gas Prices (2016).
7. Cary (n.d.).
8. Zsidisin (2007).
9. KOMATSU Company History (2007).
10. KOMATSU Company History (2007).
11. Smith (2009).

12. Tencer (2009); Dugan and Macdonald (2009).

13. *The Economist* (2011).

14. Today in Energy (2012).

15. Krauss (2016).

16. Petroleum and Other Liquids Spot Prices (n.d.).

Chapter 3

1. Chen (2010).

2. Types of Wheat (2011).

3. Natural Gas Prices (2016).

4. Natural Gas Prices (2016).

5. Natural Gas Prices (2016).

6. Natural Gas Prices (2016).

7. Natural Gas Prices (2016).

8. Natural Gas Prices (2016).

9. Natural Gas Prices (2016).

10. Trigg (1964).

Chapter 4

1. USDA Agricultural Projections to 2025 (2010).

2. Zsidisin (2005).

3. Natural Gas Annual 2014 (2015).

4. Natural Gas Supply (2016).

5. What is Shale Gas and Why is it Important? (2011).

6. Bray (2011).

7. Lithium (2015).

8. Romero (2004).

9. Corn—World Supply and Demand Summary (n.d.).

10. About Cocoa (n.d.).

11. Lithium (2015).

12. U.S. Annual Energy Outlook 2015: With Projections to 2040 (2015).

13. U.S. Annual Energy Outlook 2015: With Projections to 2040 (2015).

14. Shale Gas (n.d.).

15. Global Climate Change Indicators (n.d.).

16. Feed Grains Database: Yearbook Tables (n.d.).

17. Haley (2015).

18. New China Air Pollution Laws May Hit Aluminum Ingredient (2015).

19. Kramer (2010).

20. Ballard (2016).

21. Natural Gas Supply (2016).

22. U.S. Annual Energy Outlook: With Projections to 2040 (2015).

23. Natural Gas Consumption by End Use (n.d.).

24. Krauss (2016).

25. Worsnip (2011).

26. Henshaw (2009).

27. Craymer (2015).

28. Wheat Farmers Beef About Atkins Diet (2009).

29. World Agricultural Supply and Demand Estimates (2016).

30. World Agricultural Supply and Demand Estimates (2016).

31. World Agricultural Supply and Demand Estimates (2016).

32. World Agricultural Supply and Demand Estimates (2016).

33. Copper's Volatility Linked to Fund Activity, Not Fundamentals (2009).

34. Corn Futures (n.d.).

Chapter 5

1. Matthews (2011).

2. Zsidisin (2005).

3. Schlosser and Zsidisin (2004).

4. Corn Futures (n.d.).

5. Corn Futures (n.d.).

6. Performance Bonds/Margin Requirements (n.d.).

7. Performance Bonds/Margin Requirements (n.d.).

8. How Can I Hedge Against Rising Diesel Prices? (n.d.).

9. Schlosser and Zsidisin (2004).

10. Schlosser and Zsidisin (2004).

11. Arrowhead Develops Super-Light Bottles (2007).

Chapter 6

1. Schlosser and Zsidisin (2004).

2. Matthews (2011).

3. Copper Historical Data (2016).

4. Helman (2015).

Chapter 7

1. *The Economist* (2012).

2. Whittington (2012).

3. Kaufmann, Carter, and Rauer (2016).

4. IUPAC (2005).

5. Hensel (2011); U.S. DOE (2011).

6. Humphries (2012); U.S. DOE (2011).

7. Morrison and Tang (2012); U.S. Geological Survey (2013).

8. U.S. DOE (2011).

9. U.S. DOE (2011).

10. Spiegel International (2011).

11. Financial Times (2014); WTO (2012).

12. Reuters (2015).

13. Gulati and Sytch (2007); Liu et al. (2012).

14. European Commission (2010); U.S. Geological Survey (2013).

15. Amnesty International (2016).

Chapter 8

1. Trading Economics (2016).

2. Trading Economics (2016).

3. Tang and Zhu (2016).

4. *The Economist* (2014).

5. Tang and Zhu (2016).

6. Bloomberg News (2014).

7. KPMG (2014).

Chapter 9

1. Kolb and Overdahl (2010).

2. Schofield (2007).

References

About Cocoa. n.d. "International Cocoa Organization." Retrieved June 7, 2016 from www.icco.org/about-cocoa/growing-cocoa.html

Amnesty International. January 19, 2016. "Exposed: Child Labour Behind Smart Phone and Electric Car Batteries." Retrieved June 24, 2016 from www.amnesty.org/en/latest/news/2016/01/child-labour-behind-smart-phone-and-electric-car-batteries/

Arrowhead Develops Super-Light Bottles. 2007. *Design News* 62, no. 15, p. 36.

Ballard, E. 2016. "Sugar Industry Headed for a Shake-Up." *The Wall Street Journal*, May 17. Retrieved June 7, 2016 from www.wsj.com/articles/sugar-industry-headed-for-a-shake-up-1463464802

Bloomberg News. 2014. "China Trust Asset Growth Slows in Shadow Banking Campaign." Retrieved July 8, 2016 from www.bloomberg.com/news/articles/2014-08-12/china-s-trust-asset-growth-slows-amid-shadow-banking-crackdown

Bray, E. January 2016. "Mineral Industrial Surveys: Aluminum." U.S. Geological Survey. Retrieved July 10, 2010 from http://minerals.usgs.gov/minerals/pubs/commodity/aluminum/mcs-2016-alumi.pdf

Brent Crude Oil Historical Data. 2007–2016. "Trading Economics." Retrieved July 18, 2016 from www.tradingeconomics.com/commodity/brent-crude-oil

Brown, O., A. Crawford, and J. Gibson. 2008. "Boom or Bust: How Commodity Price Volatility Impedes Poverty Reduction, and What to Do About It." International Institute for Sustainable Development. Retrieved June 1, 2011 from www.iisd.org/pdf/2008/boom_or_bust_commodity.pdf

Cary, M. n.d. "Determining Risk Appetite." Continuity Central. Retrieved July 6, 2011 from www.continuitycentral.com/feature0170.htm

Chen, J. 2010. *Essentials of Technical Analysis for Financial Markets*. Hoboken, NJ: John Wiley and Sons.

Christian, J. 2011. "Why Silver Rose and Fell, and Why It Will Remain Volatile." *Inside Supply Management* 22, no. 5, p. 23.

Clifford, S. 2011. "Devilish Packaging, Tamed." *New York Times*, June 2. Retrieved July 22, 2011 from www.nytimes.com/2011/06/02/business/energy-environment/02packaging.html

Copper Historical Data. 2016. Investing.com. Retrieved February 15, 2016 from www.investing.com/commodities/copper-historical-data

Copper's Volatility Linked to Fund Activity, Not Fundamentals. July 1, 2009. Metal Bulletin. Retrieved July 12, 2011 from www.metalbulletin.com/Article/2245007/AMM-Coppers-volatility-linked-to-fund-activity-not-fundamentals.html

CORDIS (Community Research and Development Information Service). n.d. "The Polecat Project: Economical Exploitation of Polymer Coated Steel Sheet in Large-Scale Production of New Can Types by the European Can Industry." Retrieved July 5, 2016 from http://cordis.europa.eu/project/rcn/74401_en.html

Corn Futures. n.d. CME Group. Retrieved July 11, 2011 from www.cmegroup.com/trading/agricultural/grain-and-oilseed/corn.html

Corn—World Supply and Demand Summary. n.d. Spectrum Commodities. Retrieved July 12, 2011 from www.spectrumcommodities.com/education/commodity/statistics/corn.html

Craymer, L. 2015. "China's Changing Tastes Offer Upside for Coffee." *The Wall Street Journal*, September 16. Retrieved June 7, 2016 from www.wsj.com/articles/chinas-changing-tastes-offer-upside-for-coffee-1442431980

Dugan, I.J., and A. Macdonald. 2009. "Traders Blamed for Oil Spike." *The Wall Street Journal*, B3, July 28.

European Commission. 2010. "Critical Raw Materials for the EU. Report of the Ad-hoc Working Group on Defining Critical Raw Materials." Retrieved June 24, 2016 from https://ec.europa.eu/growth/tools-databases/eip-raw-materials/en/community/document/critical-raw-materials-eu-report-ad-hoc-working-group-defining-critical-raw

Feed Grains Database: Yearbook Tables. n.d. U.S. Department of Agriculture Economic Research Service. Retrieved February 15, 2016 from www.ers.usda.gov/data-products/feed-grains-database/feed-grains-yearbook-tables.aspx

Financial Times. March 26, 2014. "WTO Rules Against China on 'Rare Earths' Export Restrictions." Retrieved June 24, 2016 from www.ft.com/content/962a0ba4-b4e6-11e3-9166-00144feabdc0

Gaudenzi, B., G. Zsidisin, J. Hartley, and L. Kaufmann. 2015. *La Gestione Dei Commodity Price Risks: Il Punto Di Vista Della Supply Chain*. Milan, Italy: Franco Angeli. ISBN 978-88-917-0795-6

Global Climate Change Indicators. n.d. National Oceanic and Atmospheric Administration. Retrieved July 19, 2011 from www.ncdc.noaa.gov/extremes/nacem/

Gulati, R., and M. Sytch. 2007. "Dependence Asymmetry and Joint Dependence in Interorganizational Relationships: Effects of Embeddedness on a Manufacturer's Performance in Procurement Relationships." *Administrative Science Quarterly* 52, no. 1, pp. 32–69.

Haley, S. January 2015. "Projecting World Raw Sugar Prices." United States Department of Agriculture Economic Research Service. Retrieved June 7, 2016 from www.ers.usda.gov/media/1737884/sssm-317-01.pdf

Helman, C. 2015. "How Cheap Oil has Delta Airlines Jet Fooled." *Forbes.* www.forbes.com/sites/christopherhelman/2015/01/21/how-cheap-oil-has-delta-air-lines-jet-fooled/

Henry Hub Natural Gas Futures. n.d. CME Group. Retrieved July 22, 2011 from www.cmegroup.com/trading/energy/natural-gas/natural-gas_contractSpecs_futures.html

Hensel, N.D. 2011. "Economic Challenges in the Clean Energy Supply Chain: the Market for Rare Earth Minerals and Other Critical Inputs." *Business Economics* 46, no. 3, pp. 171–84.

Henshaw, C. 2009. "Woolly Logic Sees the Price of Clothes Group." *The Wall Street Journal,* June 9. Retrieved July 14, 2011 from http://blogs.wsj.com/source/2011/06/09/woolly-logic-sees-the-price-of-clothes-go-up/?mod=google_news_blog

How Can I Hedge Against Rising Diesel Prices? n.d. Investopedia. Retrieved July 26, 2011 from www.investopedia.com/ask/answers/05/dieselfutures.asp

Humphries, M. 2012. "Rare Earth Elements: The Global Supply Chain." U.S. Congressional Research Service. www.fas.org/sgp/crs/natsec/R41347.pdf

IUPAC (International Union of Pure and Applied Chemistry). 2005. *Nomenclature of Inorganic Chemistry: IUPAC Recommendations.* Cambridge, UK: RSC Publishing.

Kaufmann, L., C.R. Carter, and J. Rauer. May 2016. "The Coevolution of Relationship Dominant Logic and Supply Risk Mitigation Strategies." *Journal of Business Logistics* 37, no. 2, pp. 87–106. doi:10.1111/jbl.12126

Kellogg's 2010 Annual Report. 2010. Kellogg. Retrieved July 22, 2011 from http://investor.kelloggs.com/~/media/Files/K/Kellogg-IR/Annual%20Reports/kelloggs-2010-ar.pdf

Kolb, R.W., and J.A. Overdahl. 2010. *Financial Derivatives: Pricing and Risk Management.* Hoboken, NJ: John Wiley & Sons.

KOMATSU Company History. 2007. Sage Concepts. Retrieved July 6, 2011 from www.sageconceptsonline.com/docs/SI07CH01print.pdf

KPMG. 2014. "Shanghai Chaori: The Restructuring of China's First Domestic Bond Default." www.kpmg.com/CN/en/IssuesAndInsights/ArticlesPublications/Newsletters/restructuring-newsletter/Documents/restructuring-newsletter-1412-02-Shanghai-Chaori.pdf

Kramer, A.E. 2010. "Russia, Crippled by Drought, Bans Brain Exports." *The New York Times,* August 5. Retrieved July 17, 2016 from www.nytimes.com/2010/08/06/world/europe/06russia.html?_r=1

Krauss, C. 2016. "Oil Prices Explained: Signs of a Models Revival." *The New York Times*, June 2. Retrieved June 24, 2016 from www.nytimes.com/interactive/2016/business/energy-environment/oil-prices.html?_r=0

Lithium. 2015. U.S. Geological Survey. Retrieved June 7, 2016 from http://minerals.usgs.gov/minerals/pubs/commodity/lithium/mcs-2015-lithi.pdf

Liu, Y., Y. Huang, Y. Luo, and Y. Zhao. 2012. "How Does Justice Matter in Achieving Buyer–Supplier Relationship Performance?" *Journal of Operations Management* 30, no. 5, pp. 355–67.

Martin, H. 2011. "Rising Fuel Prices Could Cost Airlines $500 Million in Profits, Group Says." *Los Angeles Times,* March 3. Retrieved June 6, 2011 from http://articles.latimes.com/2011/mar/03/business/la-fi-0303-airline-fuel-20110303

Matthews, R.G. 2011. "Steel-Prices Increases Creep into Supply Chain." *The Wall Street Journal,* February 3. Retrieved June 28, 2011 from http://online.wsj.com/article/SB10001424052748704775604576120382801078352.html

Morrison, W.M., and R. Tang. April 30, 2012. "China's Rare Earth Industry and Export Regime: Economic and Trade Implications for the United States." U.S. Congressional Research Service. Retrieved February, 2016 from www.fas.org/sgp/crs/row/R42510.pdf

Natural Gas Annual. 2014. September 2015. U.S. Energy Information Administration. Retrieved June 7, 2016 from www.eia.gov/naturalgas/annual/

Natural Gas Consumption by End Use. n.d. U.S. Energy Information Administration. Retrieved June 7, 2016 from www.eia.gov/dnav/ng/ng_cons_sum_dcu_nus_a.htm

Natural Gas Prices. 2016. U.S. Energy Information Administration. Retrieved June 7, 2016 from www.eia.gov/dnav/ng/ng_pri_sum_a_EPG0_PG1_DMcf_m.htm

Natural Gas Spot and Futures Prices (NYMEX). n.d. U.S. Energy Information Administration. Retrieved February 15, 2016 from www.eia.gov/dnav/ng/ng_pri_fut_s1_d.htm

Natural Gas Supply. 2016. U.S. Energy Information Administration. Retrieved February 15, 2016 from www.eia.gov/naturalgas/data.cfm#consumption

New China Air Pollution Laws May Hit Aluminum Ingredient. September 25, 2015. Reuters. Retrieved June 7, 2016 from www.reuters.com/article/us-china-petcoke-regulations-idUSKCN0RP0X920150925

Pandit, K., and H. Marmanis. 2008. *Spend Analysis: The Window into Strategic Sourcing.* Ft. Lauderdale, FL: J. Ross.

Performance Bonds/Margin Requirements for CME Group Products. n.d. CME Group. Retrieved July 26, 2011 from www.cmegroup.com/clearing/margins/

Petroleum and Other Liquids Spot Prices. n.d. U.S. Energy Information Administration. Retrieved February 15, 2016 from www.eia.gov/dnav/pet/ hist/LeafHandler.ashx?n=pet&s=rwtc&f=a

Reed, D. July 24, 2008. "Can Fuel Hedging Keep Southwest in the Money?" USA Today. Retrieved June 1, 2011 from http://usatoday30.usatoday.com/ money/industries/travel/2008-07-23-southwest-jet-fuel_N.htm

Reuters. 2015. "China Abolishes Rare Earth Export Quotas: State Media." Retrieved June 24, 2016 from www.reuters.com/article/2015/01/05/us-china-rareearths-idUSKBN0KE07P20150105

Romero, S. 2004. "Trinidad Becomes a Natural Gas Giant." *The New York Times*, October 13. Retrieved September 17, 2016 from http://www.nytimes. com/2004/10/13/business/worldbusiness/trinidad-becomes-a-natural-gas-giant.html?_r=0

Schlosser, M.A., and G.A. Zsidisin. 2004. "Hedging Fuel Surcharge Price Fluctuations." *Practix: Good Practices in Purchasing and Supply Chain Management*. www.capsresearch.org

Schofield, N.C. 2007. *Commodity Derivatives: Markets and Applications*. Chichester, England: John Wiley & Sons.

Shale Gas. n.d. U.S. Energy Information Administration. Retrieved June 7, 2016 from www.eia.gov/dnav/ng/NG_ENR_SHALEGAS_A_EPG0_R5301_ BCF_A.htm

Skybus Airlines to Cease Operations. April 4, 2008. USA Today. Retrieved June 2, 2011 from www.usatoday.com/travel/news/2008-04-04-skybus-shutdown_N.htm

Smith, J.L. November 6, 2009. "The 2008 Oil Price Shock: Markets or Mayhem?" Resources for the Future. Retrieved July 6, 2011 from www.rff. org/blog/2009/2008-oil-price-shock-markets-or-mayhem

Spiegel International. November 2, 2011. "Help for German Industry: Merkel Joins the Global Hunt for Natural Resources." Retrieved June 24, 2016 from www.spiegel.de/international/world/help-for-german-industry-merkel-joins-the-global-hunt-for-natural-resources-a-795256.html

Tang, K., and H. Zhu. 2016. "Commodities as Collateral." Retrieved July 8, 2016 from www.mit.edu/~zhuh/TangZhu_CommodityCollateral.pdf

Tencer, D. July 29, 2009. "CFTC: Speculators Caused 2008 Oil Price Crisis." Alex Jones' Prison Planet. Retrieved July 24, 2011 from www.prison planet. com/cftc-speculators-caused-2008-oil-price-crisis.html

The Economist. 2014. "China's Shadow Banks. A Moving Target." Retrieved July 8, 2016 from www.economist.com/news/finance-and-economics/21615625-chinas-shape-shifting-shadow-banks-evolve-once-more-moving-target

The Economist. March 3, 2011. "The 2011 Oil Shock." Retrieved June 24, 2015 from www.economist.com/node/18281774

The Economist. January 21, 2012. "The Visible Hand." Special Report. Retrieved June 24, 2016 from www.economist.com/node/21542931

The Silver Institute. 2011. Retrieved July 5, 2016 from www.silverinstitute.org/site/wp-content/uploads/2011/06/WSS2016Summary.pdf

Today in Energy. August 21, 2012. "Crude Oil Prices Peaked Early in 2012." U.S. Energy Information Administration. Retrieved June 24, 2016 from www.eia.gov/todayinenergy/detail.cfm?id=7630

Trading Economics. 2016. "Soybeans Trends 1959–2016." Retrieved July 8, 2016 from www.tradingeconomics.com/commodity/soybeans

Trigg, D.W. 1964. "Monitoring a Forecasting System." *Operational Research Quarterly* 15, no. 3, pp. 271–74.

Tseng, N. January 21, 2011. "Three Challenges to McDonald's Growth." CNN Money. Retrieved June 1, 2011 from http://archive.fortune.com/2011/01/21/news/companies/mcdonalds_slowing_growth.fortune/index.htm

Turner, P.A., and S.H. Lim. 2015. "Hedging Jet Fuel Price Risk: The Case of U.S. Passenger Airlines." *Journal of Air Transport* 44, pp. 54–64.

Types of Wheat. 2011. "Texas Wheat Producers Board and Association." Retrieved July 19, 2011 from http://texaswheat.org/wp-content/uploads/2014/06/6-classes-of-wheat.pdf

U.S. Annual Energy Outlook 2015: With Projections to 2040. April 2015. U.S. Energy Information Administration. Retrieved June 7, 2016 from www.eia.gov/forecasts/aeo/pdf/0383%282015%29.pdf

U.S. DOE (U.S. Department of Energy). December 2011. "Critical Materials Strategy." Retrieved June 24, 2016 from www.energy.gov/node/349057

U.S. Geological Survey. 2013. "Mineral Commodity Summaries 2013." Retrieved June 24, 2016 from http://minerals.usgs.gov/minerals/pubs/mcs/2013/mcs2013.pdf

USDA Agricultural Projections to 2025. February 2010. U.S. Department of Agriculture. Retrieved February 15, 2016 from www.usda.gov/oce/commodity/projections/USDA_Agricultural_Projections_to_2025.pdf

Web Tool: Strategic Profit Model. n.d. Institute for Supply Management. Retrieved July 22, 2011 from www.ism.ws/ismapps/cavinato/prtver.cfm

What is Shale Gas and Why is it Important? April 2011. U.S. Energy Information Administration. Retrieved July 10, 2011 from www.eia.gov/energy_in_brief/about_shale_gas.cfm

Wheat Farmers Beef About Atkins Diet. February 11, 2009. *CBS News.* Retrieved July 10, 2011 from www.cbsnews.com/stories/2003/04/28/health/main551336.shtml

Whittington, R. 2012. "Big Strategy/Small Strategy." *Strategic Organization* 10, no. 3, pp. 263–68.

World Agricultural Supply and Demand Estimates. May 10, 2016. United States Department of Agriculture. Retrieved June 7, 2016 from www.usda.gov/oce/commodity/wasde/latest.pdf

Worsnip, P. May 3, 2011. "World Population to Pass 7 Billion on October 31." Reuters. Retrieved July 14, 2011 from www.reuters.com/article/2011/05/03/us-un-population-idUSTRE7426GI20110503

WTO (World Trade Organization). 2012. "China—Measures Related to the Exportation of Rare Earths, Tungsten and Molybdenum." Retrieved June 24, 2016 from www.wto.org/english/tratop_e/dispu_e/cases_e/ds431_e.htm

Zsidisin, G.A. 2005. "Managing Commodity Spend in Turbulent Times." CAPS Research. Retrieved July 6, 2011 from www.capsresearch.org/publications/pdfs-protected/cir062005.pdf

Zsidisin, G.A. 2007. "Business and Supply Chain Continuity." CAPS Research. Retrieved July 6, 2011 from www.capsresearch.org/publications/pdfs-protected/cir012007.pdf

Zsidisin, G.A., J.L. Hartley, and L. Kaufmann. 2013. *Management von Rohstoffpreisrisiken: Ein Supply Chain Perspektive.* Vallender, Germany: European Management Publications. ISBN 978-3-938877-30-2

Zsidisin, G.A., J.L. Hartley, L. Kaufmann, and B. Gaudenzi. 2014. "Managing Commodity Price Volatility and Risk." CAPS Research. ISBN 978-1-940404-01-1

Index

OTHER TITLES IN OUR SUPPLY AND OPERATIONS MANAGEMENT COLLECTION

Joy M. Field, Boston College, Editor

- *Better Business Decisions Using Cost Modeling, Second Edition* by Victor Sower and Christopher Sower
- *Improving Business Performance with Lean, Second Edition* by James R. Bradley
- *Lean Communication: Applications for Continuous Process Improvement* by Sam Yankelevitch and Claire F. Kuhl
- *Leading and Managing Lean* by Gene Fliedner
- *Mapping Workflows and Managing Knowledge, Volume I: Using Formal and Tacit Knowledge to Improve Organizational Performance* by John L. Kmetz
- *Mapping Workflows and Managing Knowledge, Volume II: Dynamic Modeling of Formal and Tacit Knowledge to Improve Organizational Performance* by John L. Kmetz
- *Managing and Improving Quality: Integrating Quality, Statistical Methods and Process Control* by Amar Sahay
- *An Introduction to Lean Work Design: Fundamentals of Lean Operations, Volume I* by Lawrence D. Fredendall and Matthias Thürer
- *An Introduction to Lean Work Design: Standard Practices and Tools of Lean, Volume II* by Lawrence D. Fredendall and Matthias Thürer

Announcing the Business Expert Press Digital Library

Concise e-books business students need for classroom and research

This book can also be purchased in an e-book collection by your library as

- a one-time purchase,
- that is owned forever,
- allows for simultaneous readers,
- has no restrictions on printing, and
- can be downloaded as PDFs from within the library community.

Our digital library collections are a great solution to beat the rising cost of textbooks. E-books can be loaded into their course management systems or onto students' e-book readers.

The **Business Expert Press** digital libraries are very affordable, with no obligation to buy in future years. For more information, please visit **www.businessexpertpress.com/librarians**. To set up a trial in the United States, please email **sales@businessexpertpress.com**.

CPSIA information can be obtained
at www.ICGtesting.com
Printed in the USA
LVOW01s0121111216

516756LV00005B/57/P